The Smart Living Trust Guide

How to Create Your Own Trust, Avoid Probate and Protect a Legacy Without Confusion

DR. MIKE BRANDON

Harbour House Press

harbourhousepublishing.com

Table of Contents

Table of Contents....2
Introduction....4
The Power of Living Trusts....4
Chapter 1....9
Understanding Living Trusts....9
Chapter 2....17
Debunking Common Living Trust Misconceptions....17
Chapter 3....22
For Love & Money: Why Creating a Living Trust Matters 22
Chapter 4....31
Building Your Living Trust....31
Chapter 5....44
Understanding Taxes and Living Trusts....44
Chapter 6....58
Updating Your Living Trust....58
Chapter 7....68
Risks, Limitations & Drawbacks....68
Chapter 8....80
How Living Trusts Impact Beneficiaries....80
How Asset Distribution Works....80
Chapter 9....87
Living Trusts In The Modern World....87
Chapter 10....93
What Happens After Death?....93
About the Author....111
References & Citations....112
Author's Note on Citations....114

Introduction

The Power of Living Trusts

In the world of financial and estate planning, the words of Benjamin Franklin still ring true: *"By failing to prepare, you are preparing to fail."* Few areas of life prove this more clearly than planning for what happens to your assets, your family, and your legacy when you are no longer able to manage them yourself.

Imagine a family gathered after the passing of a loved one. Instead of confusion, tension, or disputes over "what would have been wanted," there is clarity. Decisions are understood. Transitions are smooth. Relationships remain intact.

This kind of outcome rarely happens by accident.

More often, it is the result of thoughtful estate planning—and in many cases, the use of a properly structured living trust. A living trust can transform what might otherwise be a stressful, costly, and emotionally charged process into a private, orderly transfer of responsibility and assets.

Estate planning is not only about preserving wealth. It is also about preserving peace. When done correctly, it reduces uncertainty, limits conflict, and allows your family to focus on healing rather than paperwork and court procedures.

At the heart of this book is a simple mission: to help you understand living trusts clearly and confidently. This is not just about avoiding probate or protecting property. It is about giving you the knowledge and tools to shape your legacy on your own terms. Whether your goal is to protect your heirs, maintain privacy, minimize delays, or ensure your wishes are carried out exactly as intended, this guide is designed to put you on the right path.

Cutting Through the Confusion

Estate planning often feels overwhelming because it is filled with legal terminology, conflicting advice, and unnecessary complexity. This book takes a different approach.

In the chapters ahead, we break down living trusts in plain language and explain how they work in practical, real-world terms. One of the most well-known benefits of a living trust is the ability to avoid probate—the court-supervised process that can delay asset distribution, increase costs, and expose private financial details to the public.

By avoiding probate, a living trust can help your estate pass to your beneficiaries more quickly, more privately, and often with fewer expenses. It can also reduce the likelihood of disputes by clearly documenting your intentions and putting a structured plan in place.

You'll also learn how living trusts interact with taxes, what they can and cannot accomplish, and how proper planning can help preserve more of what you've worked hard to build. Throughout the book, you'll find practical explanations, examples, and guidance you can actually use—whether your priorities include protecting minor children, planning for incapacity, supporting loved ones, or ensuring a smooth transition of a family business.

By the end of this guide, you should feel confident in your understanding of living trusts and your ability to make informed decisions about whether—and how—to use one. The goal is peace of mind: knowing that what matters most to you is protected.

Setting the Stage for Understanding Living Trusts

Before exploring the details of living trusts, it's important to understand the perspective behind this book. Effective estate planning requires not just information, but clarity, responsibility, and practical insight.

This guide is written from the standpoint of professionals who have spent years studying, implementing, and explaining estate planning strategies, including living trusts. The insights shared here are drawn from extensive experience in financial planning, retirement preparation, and trust-based estate solutions.

Rather than overwhelming you with legal theory, this book focuses on practical understanding—what living trusts are, how they work, where they help, and where their limitations lie. The goal is not to replace professional legal advice, but to help you become an informed, confident participant in your own planning process.

As you move through the chapters, you can trust that the guidance provided is grounded in real-world application and a commitment to helping individuals and families make thoughtful, well-informed decisions about their futures.

Your Guide Through the Estate Planning Journey

You are not expected to be an expert before you begin reading this book. Each section is designed to build understanding step by step, turning complex ideas into clear, manageable concepts. Whether you are just starting to think about estate planning or refining an existing plan, this guide is meant to support you at every stage.

Securing Your Future With Confidence

As you continue, remember that this book is about more than documents and legal structures. It is about protecting your future, preserving your values, and providing clarity and care for the people you love. With thoughtful planning and the right tools, you can leave behind not confusion—but confidence.

Chapter 1

Understanding Living Trusts

"A man who does not plan long ahead will find trouble at his door." —Confucius

The Basics of Living Trusts

Every effective estate plan begins with a clear understanding of its core tools. One of the most practical and widely used of these tools is the living trust. Living trusts offer a flexible, efficient way to manage assets, protect loved ones, and ensure that your wishes are carried out with minimal disruption.

Contrary to popular belief, living trusts are not reserved for the wealthy. They are accessible, adaptable, and useful for individuals and families at many stages of life. Whether your estate is simple or complex, a living trust can play a valuable role in your overall planning strategy.

What Is a Living Trust?

A living trust is a legal arrangement in which assets are placed under the management of a trustee for the benefit of one or more beneficiaries. Unlike a will, a living trust becomes effective during your lifetime, allowing you to manage and control your assets while you are alive and capable.

As the person who creates the trust—often called the trustmaker or grantor—you decide how the assets are managed, who benefits from them, and when distributions occur. These assets can include bank accounts, investments, real estate, business interests, and personal property.

One of the primary advantages of a living trust is its ability to avoid probate. Probate is a court-supervised process used to validate a will and distribute assets after death. It can be time-consuming, costly, and public. Assets held in a properly funded living trust typically pass directly to beneficiaries without going through probate, allowing for faster and more private transfers.

Living trusts also provide continuity. If you become incapacitated, the trustee can step in and manage the trust assets without the need for court intervention. This feature alone makes living trusts an important planning tool for many families.

Different Lives, Different Types of Trusts

Living trusts are not one-size-fits-all solutions. They come in several forms, each designed to meet different planning goals and personal circumstances.

The two most common types are **revocable** and **irrevocable** living trusts.

A **revocable living trust** allows you to retain control over the assets in the trust during your lifetime. You can amend, update, or revoke the trust as your needs change. Because of this flexibility, revocable trusts are the most commonly used type of living trust in estate planning.

An **irrevocable living trust**, once established, generally cannot be changed. While this lack of flexibility may seem limiting, irrevocable trusts can offer advantages in asset protection and tax planning. Assets placed in an irrevocable trust are typically no longer considered part of your personal estate, which can provide protection from creditors and help reduce estate taxes in certain situations.

There are also specialized trusts designed for specific needs. A **special needs trust**, for example, can provide ongoing support for a beneficiary with disabilities without jeopardizing eligibility for government assistance. A **minor's trust** allows assets to be managed responsibly for children until they reach an age or milestone you choose.

Charitable trusts, business succession trusts, and other specialized arrangements further demonstrate how adaptable living trusts can be. No matter the sizc or complexity of an estate, there is often a trust structure that can support the desired outcome.

The Purpose and Benefits of a Living Trust

Living trusts serve several important purposes in modern estate planning. The most widely recognized benefit is probate avoidance, but the advantages go well beyond that.

Living trusts provide privacy. Because trust assets generally do not pass through probate, the details of your estate are not made part of the public record.

They also offer control. A living trust allows you to decide how and when assets are distributed, which can be especially important when beneficiaries are young, financially inexperienced, or in need of long-term support.

Another significant benefit is incapacity planning. If you become unable to manage your affairs, a successor trustee can step in immediately to manage trust assets according to your instructions, avoiding the need for court-appointed guardians or conservators.

Flexibility is another key advantage. Most living trusts can be modified as your life circumstances change, allowing your estate plan to evolve along with your needs.

Ultimately, a living trust provides structure, clarity, and continuity—three elements that help reduce uncertainty and protect both assets and relationships.

The Core Components of a Living Trust

The Trust Agreement

The trust agreement is the foundation of a living trust. It is the legal document that outlines how the trust operates and how assets are managed and distributed.

A well-drafted trust agreement typically:

- Specifies how and when assets are distributed to beneficiaries

- Names the trustee and successor trustees
- Defines the trustee's authority and responsibilities
- Explains how the trust can be amended or revoked (if applicable)
- Establishes procedures for trustee replacement
- Includes special provisions for minors, dependents, or beneficiaries with special needs

This document serves as a roadmap for trustees and helps ensure that your intentions are clearly understood and properly carried out.

The Trust Property

The assets placed into a living trust—often referred to as trust property—form the working substance of the trust. A living trust can hold many types of assets, including:

- **Real estate**, such as a primary residence, rental property, or land
- **Bank and investment accounts**, including savings, checking, and brokerage accounts
- **Personal property**, such as vehicles, jewelry, artwork, and collectibles
- **Business interests**, including ownership in closely held businesses, partnerships, or LLCs
- **Life insurance**, when structured appropriately within the estate plan
- **Intellectual property**, such as copyrights, patents, and trademarks

Properly transferring assets into the trust—often called "funding" the trust—is essential. Assets not titled in the trust may still be subject to probate.

The Beneficiaries

Beneficiaries are the individuals or organizations who receive the benefits of the trust. Protecting and providing for beneficiaries is at the heart of every living trust.

Living trusts allow for:

- Direct and efficient asset distribution
- Customized timing and conditions for inheritances
- Privacy in asset transfers
- Continued asset management in cases of incapacity
- Structured protection for beneficiaries from poor financial decisions or outside pressures

By thoughtfully selecting beneficiaries and tailoring provisions to their needs, a living trust becomes a powerful tool for long-term planning and peace of mind.

Key People Involved in a Living Trust

You, the Trustmaker: The Visionary Planner

Every living trust begins with you—the trustmaker. This is the person who initiates the estate planning process by deciding how their assets will be managed and eventually distributed. Taking this proactive step is not just about protecting your financial future, but also about securing the well-being of those you care about most.

Starting early gives you the advantage of time: time to thoughtfully consider your wishes, refine your plan, and adjust as your circumstances change.

Beyond the practical benefits, being the trustmaker brings peace of mind. With a well-crafted living trust in place, you know your assets will be protected, your loved ones supported, and your intentions respected—without the need for court involvement.

The Trustee: The Trusted Manager

The trustee plays a critical role as the steward of your living trust. Charged with managing the trust's assets and carrying out your instructions, the trustee must be responsible, detail-oriented, and committed to acting in the best interests of the beneficiaries.

Key trustee responsibilities include:

- **Asset Management:** Overseeing and prudently managing trust assets, including investing wisely, maintaining property, and keeping accurate records of all transactions.
- **Distribution of Assets:** Disbursing assets to beneficiaries according to the terms of the trust, whether through scheduled payments or conditional distributions such as funding education.
- **Tax Compliance:** Handling all necessary tax filings and payments related to the trust.
- **Fiduciary Duty:** Acting with integrity and loyalty, placing beneficiaries' interests above their own and avoiding conflicts of interest.

To fulfill these duties effectively, trustees should also:

- Maintain clear, ongoing communication with beneficiaries to set expectations and reduce conflicts.

- Keep thorough documentation of all trust-related decisions and actions for transparency and accountability.
- Consult with legal, financial, and tax professionals when needed to ensure proper management.

By embodying these qualities, the trustee safeguards your legacy and protects the future of your beneficiaries.

Key Takeaways

- **Understanding the Basics:** A strong grasp of living trust fundamentals is essential for effective estate planning.
- **Empowerment Through Planning:** As trustmaker, you take control of your legacy, planning proactively to provide for those you care about.
- **Strategic Asset Management:** A living trust's flexibility allows for a diverse range of assets to be included, making it adaptable to your unique needs and goals.
- **The Trustee's Role:** Choosing a trustworthy and diligent trustee is crucial, as they carry the responsibility of honoring your wishes and managing the estate responsibly.
- **Estate Planning for Everyone:** Living trusts are accessible tools that can benefit individuals at various life stages and financial levels.

Chapter 2
Debunking Common Living Trust Misconceptions

"Knowledge is power. Information is liberating. Education is the premise of progress, in every society, in every family."— Kofi Annan

You Don't Have to Be Wealthy to Benefit from a Living Trust

Living trusts were once seen as tools only for the wealthy or famous. Today, that's simply not true. Living trusts have become a practical, accessible estate planning tool for people across all income levels. Even modest estates can gain significant advantages from having a living trust in place. In fact, many middle-income families find living trusts to be an essential part of their financial planning.

The Cost Myth: Are Living Trusts Expensive?

Is creating a living trust expensive? Not necessarily. While there is an upfront investment, the cost is often justified by the long-term benefits and savings. Here's what to consider:

- **Initial Setup Costs:** The expense of establishing a living trust varies depending on the complexity of your estate and whether you hire a professional. Attorney fees typically range from a few hundred to a few thousand dollars. Though this may seem like a significant cost, it's often small compared to the savings on probate fees, legal costs, and court expenses down the road.

- **Do-It-Yourself Options:** For those with straightforward estates or limited budgets, online services and software can offer affordable DIY living trust templates—usually costing between $50 and $300. However, it's important to ensure any DIY trust complies with your state's laws and fits your unique needs.

- **Additional Costs:** There may be minor extra expenses, such as notarization, recording fees for transferring real estate titles into the trust, and occasional updates or amendments to the trust. These ongoing costs are generally minimal compared to the initial setup.

- **Long-Term Savings:** The greatest financial benefit comes from avoiding probate—a process that can be costly, lengthy, and public. A living trust enables quicker, private asset transfers, potentially saving thousands of dollars and providing your beneficiaries access to their inheritance without delay.

In short, while there is some upfront cost, a living trust is often a wise investment that pays off in time, money, and peace of mind.

Revocable vs. Irrevocable Trusts: Understanding The Difference

Understanding the difference between irrevocable and revocable trusts is essential to choosing the right tool for your estate plan. The key distinction lies in control and flexibility after the trust is established.

Revocable Trusts

- **Flexibility:** You, as the trustmaker (or grantor), can modify, amend, or revoke the trust at any time during your lifetime. This allows you to adjust your plan as your needs and wishes evolve.
- **Control:** You maintain full control over the assets in the trust while alive.
- **Probate Avoidance:** Assets held in a revocable trust typically avoid probate, allowing for faster, private transfer to beneficiaries.
- **Incapacity Planning:** Provides a clear mechanism for managing your assets if you become incapacitated, without court involvement.
- **Privacy:** Unlike wills that go through probate and become public, revocable trusts keep your estate details private.

Limitations:

- Assets remain part of your estate for creditor claims and estate tax purposes.

- Initial setup costs apply, though these are usually balanced by probate savings.

Irrevocable Trusts

- **Asset Protection:** Once assets are transferred to an irrevocable trust, they generally are shielded from creditors and legal judgments.
- **Tax Benefits:** Transferring assets out of your estate may reduce estate taxes and qualify for gift tax exemptions.
- **Government Benefit Eligibility:** Irrevocable trusts can help beneficiaries qualify for government assistance programs, like Medicaid, by reducing countable assets.

Trade-offs:

- You relinquish control—assets placed in an irrevocable trust cannot be changed or reclaimed.
- Establishing the trust is more complex and can be costly due to detailed legal and tax considerations.
- Irrevocability means mistakes or life changes cannot be easily undone, requiring careful planning.

Making the Right Choice

Choosing between a revocable and irrevocable trust depends on your personal goals: whether you prioritize flexibility and control, asset protection, tax planning, or government benefit eligibility.

Consulting with experienced estate planning professionals can help clarify which option best suits your unique situation and objectives.

Key Takeaways

- **Accessible to All:** Living trusts benefit individuals and families across all income levels, not just the wealthy.
- **Cost-Effective:** While there is an upfront cost, living trusts often save time, money, and hassle by avoiding probate.
- **Revocable Trusts Offer Flexibility:** They allow for changes and revocation during your lifetime, maintaining your control.
- **Irrevocable Trusts Provide Asset Protection:** They offer strong protection from creditors and potential tax advantages but require permanent commitment.
- **Informed Decisions Matter:** Understanding your goals and circumstances is crucial to choosing the right type of trust.
- **Seek Professional Guidance:** Estate planning can be complex; expert advice ensures your plan aligns with your needs and complies with legal requirements.

Chapter 3

For Love & Money: Why Creating a Living Trust Matters

"An ounce of prevention is worth a pound of cure."—
Benjamin Franklin

Creating a living trust is not about fear—it's about foresight. It's about protecting the people you love, preserving what you've worked hard to build, and ensuring that your wishes are carried out smoothly, privately, and efficiently. One of the most powerful reasons people choose a living trust is simple: **to avoid probate and its many complications.**

Probate Evasion: The Great Escape

In estate planning, avoiding probate is like pulling off a flawless escape act. Probate is slow, public, expensive, and often emotionally draining for families. A living trust allows your estate to bypass this process entirely, ensuring your assets move swiftly and quietly to the people you intended.

The Pitfalls of Probate

Probate is the court-supervised process used to validate a will and distribute a deceased person's estate. While it's meant to provide structure, it often creates unnecessary burdens for grieving families.

High Costs
Probate can significantly reduce the value of an estate. Attorney fees, court costs, executor fees, and administrative expenses can consume a large portion of assets—sometimes tens of thousands of dollars—before beneficiaries receive anything.

Loss of Privacy
Probate proceedings are public record. Anyone can access details about the estate, including asset values and beneficiaries. This lack of privacy can invite unwanted attention, disputes, or creditor claims.

Lengthy Delays
Probate can take months—or even years—to complete, depending on the estate's complexity and local court procedures. During this time, heirs may be left without access to funds they urgently need.

Family Conflict
Public disclosure and delays often create tension. Disagreements among heirs can escalate into contested wills and drawn-out legal battles, straining relationships and draining estate resources.

Administrative Burden
Executors face heavy responsibilities: locating assets, settling debts, filing court paperwork, and complying with legal timelines. This process can be overwhelming, especially for family members already coping with loss.

Given these drawbacks, it's easy to see why many people seek a better alternative.

How a Living Trust Bypasses Probate

A living trust offers a streamlined, private, and efficient way to transfer assets—without court involvement.

Ownership Transfer
When assets are placed into a living trust, ownership shifts from you personally to the trust. While you remain in full control during your lifetime, those assets are no longer subject to probate at death.

Successor Trustee in Place
You appoint a successor trustee in advance. Upon your passing, this person steps in immediately to manage and distribute assets according to your instructions—no court approval required.

No Court Delays
Because trust assets are not part of the probate estate, beneficiaries don't have to wait for months or years to receive what you intended for them.

Privacy Maintained
Trust administration happens privately. Only the trustee and beneficiaries are involved, keeping family and financial matters out of the public eye.

Multi-State Simplicity
If you own property in more than one state, a living trust eliminates the need for separate probate proceedings in each jurisdiction.

Lower Overall Costs
By avoiding probate, estates often save substantial sums in legal fees, court costs, and administrative expenses—preserving more wealth for heirs.

Protecting Your Heirs: A Gift That Endures

A living trust doesn't just transfer assets—it protects them. It provides structure, safeguards inheritances, and ensures that what you leave behind benefits your loved ones as intended. With the right planning, a trust can shield beneficiaries from unnecessary legal challenges, delays, and financial uncertainty.

Avoiding Family Feuds with a Living Trust

One of the most overlooked benefits of a living trust is its ability to preserve family harmony. Clear planning today can prevent painful disputes tomorrow.

Clear Instructions Eliminate Guesswork
A well-drafted trust spells out exactly who receives what, when, and under what conditions. This clarity reduces misunderstandings and limits grounds for conflict.

Privacy Reduces Tension
Because trust distributions are private, they don't become public spectacles. This discretion helps protect family dignity and minimizes outside interference.

Blocks Unwanted Claims
By bypassing probate and clearly naming beneficiaries, a living trust reduces the risk of distant relatives or third parties attempting to challenge the estate.

Allows Thoughtful Provisions
Living trusts can accommodate unique family situations—such as providing extra care for a child with special needs or staggering distributions for younger beneficiaries—helping everyone understand that decisions were intentional and fair.

Encourages Early Clarity
Many trustmakers discuss their plans with family members while alive. These conversations foster understanding, reduce surprises, and help loved ones accept decisions in advance.

Adapts as Life Changes
Most living trusts are revocable, allowing updates as relationships, finances, or personal circumstances evolve—keeping the plan relevant and aligned with your wishes.

A Public Lesson: Aretha Franklin and the Cost of Unclear Planning

When the "Queen of Soul," **Aretha Franklin**, passed away, she left behind an extraordinary musical legacy—but no clear, legally binding will or living trust. What followed was a lengthy, public, and emotionally charged legal battle among her heirs. Despite the size and value of her estate, the absence of formal estate planning created confusion, delays, and family conflict.

Aretha Franklin's story is a sobering reminder that wealth alone does not protect a legacy. Without clear instructions, even the most successful individuals leave room for uncertainty and dispute. A properly executed living trust could have provided clarity, privacy, and direction—allowing her wishes to be honored without public scrutiny or family discord. Her experience underscores a simple truth: **preparation preserves peace**.

Immediate Asset Distribution: Because Waiting Helps No One

One of the most practical advantages of a living trust is speed. Unlike wills that must pass through probate, living trusts allow for **immediate or timely distribution of assets**.

When the trustmaker passes away, authority transfers seamlessly to the successor trustee. Because no court approval is required, asset distribution can begin almost immediately, guided solely by the instructions laid out in the trust.

This efficiency offers several critical benefits:

Timely Financial Support
Beneficiaries gain access to funds when they need them most—for living expenses, education, healthcare, or urgent obligations.

Reduced Financial Stress
The period after a loss is already emotionally taxing. A living trust removes financial uncertainty by providing clarity and access without delay.

Preservation of Asset Value
Assets such as businesses or real estate can lose value if left unmanaged. Quick distribution allows beneficiaries to take control and protect what they inherit.

Lower Administrative Costs
Probate often incurs ongoing management and maintenance expenses. Living trusts minimize or eliminate these costs by accelerating asset transfer.

In short, living trusts respect both time and need—ensuring loved ones aren't left waiting during an already difficult season.

Your Rules, Your Legacy: Control Even During Incapacity

A living trust does more than plan for death—it protects you during life.

If illness, injury, or age leaves you unable to manage your affairs, a living trust ensures continuity. You appoint a successor trustee in advance—someone you trust—to step in and manage assets according to your instructions. This avoids court-appointed conservatorships and preserves your autonomy.

Instead of uncertainty or legal delays, your affairs remain in capable hands, guided by your clearly defined wishes.

The Stan Lee Lesson: Guarding Against Undue Influence

In his later years, **Stan Lee**, the legendary creator behind Marvel Comics, reportedly faced troubling issues involving elder abuse and questionable influence over his finances and personal affairs. Despite his fame and resources, his situation revealed a hard truth: without clear safeguards, anyone can become vulnerable.

A well-structured living trust helps prevent such situations. By clearly defining who manages assets and under what conditions, a trust reduces the risk of manipulation and ensures decisions align with the trustmaker's true intentions. Stan Lee's experience serves as a reminder that estate planning is not just about wealth—it's about dignity, autonomy, and protection.

Directing Distribution: Precision with Purpose

Living trusts offer unmatched control over how assets are distributed. Unlike wills, which are subject to probate delays and challenges, trusts allow you to specify **exactly** how, when, and to whom assets are given.

Distributions can be tied to milestones—such as completing education—or structured in stages to encourage responsibility. Conditions can be set to protect beneficiaries from financial mismanagement or external pressure. This precision transforms your estate from a simple transfer of wealth into a thoughtful extension of your values.

Your legacy becomes intentional—not accidental.

The Easy-Change Advantage: Updating Your Living Trust

Revocable living trusts are designed to evolve with your life. As circumstances change—marriages, births, divorces, financial shifts, or personal priorities—your trust can be updated or even revoked.

Amendments allow you to revise beneficiaries, change trustees, or adjust distribution terms without rewriting the entire document. With proper execution, these updates are straightforward and ensure your estate plan always reflects your current intentions.

This flexibility makes revocable living trusts one of the most adaptable tools in estate planning—giving you confidence that your legacy remains aligned with who you are today.

Final Thought

A living trust is more than a legal document—it's a preventive measure rooted in love, responsibility, and wisdom. By avoiding probate, protecting privacy, and clearly expressing your intentions, you give your family something invaluable: **certainty during uncertain times.**

Key Takeaways

- **Efficient Estate Management:** Living trusts streamline asset distribution and avoid the delays and publicity of probate.
- **Time and Cost Savings:** Bypassing probate preserves estate value and reduces legal expenses.
- **Protection for Beneficiaries:** Trusts safeguard heirs from delays, disputes, and unnecessary legal exposure.
- **Family Harmony:** Clear, private instructions help prevent conflicts and misunderstandings.

- **Incapacity Planning:** Living trusts ensure your affairs are managed according to your wishes if you're unable to do so yourself.
- **Built-In Flexibility:** Revocable trusts adapt easily to life's changes, keeping your plan current and effective.

Chapter 4

Building Your Living Trust

"To accomplish great things, we must not only act but also dream; not only plan but also believe."— Anatole France

Creating The Framework Your Living Trust

Creating a living trust is one of the most intentional steps you can take to protect your assets and direct how your legacy unfolds. Think of it as designing the architectural blueprint for your estate—every line matters, and the strength of the structure depends on the clarity of the plan.

This chapter walks you through the practical process of building a living trust from the ground up. By the end, you'll understand how to create a clear, legally sound framework that reflects your wishes and stands the test of time.

Drafting Your Trust Document: The Master Plan

The trust document is the heart of your living trust. It transforms your intentions into enforceable instructions and ensures your estate is handled exactly as you envision. Precision matters here—vague language or missing details can undermine even the best intentions.

Below are the essential steps involved in drafting a strong and effective living trust:

1. **Choose the Right Type of Trust**
   Decide whether a revocable or irrevocable trust best aligns with your goals. Revocable trusts offer flexibility, allowing you to amend or revoke the trust during your lifetime. Irrevocable trusts, while permanent, may provide asset protection and tax advantages.
2. **Identify Your Beneficiaries Clearly**
   Specify exactly who will benefit from the trust. Beneficiaries may include family members, friends, charities, or organizations. Clear identification helps avoid confusion and prevents future disputes.
3. **Appoint a Trustee and Successor Trustees**
   Select a reliable individual or institution to manage the trust. Many trustmakers serve as their own trustee initially, with a successor trustee stepping in upon death or incapacity. This ensures continuity and stability.
4. **Create a Complete Asset Inventory**
   List all assets you intend to placc into the trust—real estate, bank accounts, investments, business interests, and personal property. A thorough inventory ensures nothing important is overlooked.
5. **Define Distribution Terms**
   Outline how and when assets should be distributed. You may set conditions based on age, milestones, or

specific circumstances that reflect your values and intentions.

6. **Include a Pour-Over Will**
   A pour-over will acts as a backup, directing any assets not transferred into the trust during your lifetime into the trust after death, ensuring consistency in distribution.
7. **Seek Professional Guidance**
   While some trusts can be created independently, estate planning laws are nuanced. Consulting an estate planning attorney helps ensure your trust is legally valid and tailored to your jurisdiction.
8. **Sign and Notarize the Trust**
   The trust document must be properly executed—typically signed in front of a notary—to make it legally binding.
9. **Fund the Trust**
   A trust only works if it owns assets. Funding the trust involves formally transferring ownership of assets into the trust, which varies by asset type.

Drafting a living trust requires foresight and attention to detail. When done correctly, it becomes a durable master plan that protects your estate and honors your legacy.

The Howard Hughes Estate: A Lesson in Clarity and Formalization

Howard Hughes—billionaire aviator, filmmaker, and business magnate—died in 1976 without a valid will or living trust. What followed was years of litigation, fueled by disputed handwritten documents and competing claims. The absence of formal estate planning led to confusion, conflict, and significant depletion of his estate.

Hughes' story underscores a critical truth: intentions mean little without proper documentation. A clearly drafted and legally recognized trust could have preserved his estate, avoided public battles, and ensured his wishes were carried out. His legacy serves as a cautionary reminder that clarity and formalization are not optional—they're essential.

Must-Haves for a Rock-Solid Living Trust

For a living trust to function effectively, certain foundational elements must be in place. These components ensure legal validity, operational clarity, and smooth administration:

- **Clear Declaration of Intent**
  The document must explicitly state that it creates a living trust and identify whether it is revocable or irrevocable.
- **Identification of the Trustmaker**
  Clearly name the individual establishing the trust, affirming their authority to transfer assets.
- **Appointment of a Trustee**
  Name a competent trustee and define their duties, powers, and compensation, if any.
- **Designation of Successor Trustees**
  Provide backups to ensure uninterrupted management if the original trustee can no longer serve.
- **Detailed Beneficiary Designations**
  Clearly identify beneficiaries and specify any conditions or allocations tied to their inheritance.
- **Comprehensive Asset Listing**
  Include detailed descriptions of assets held by the trust to ensure proper management and transfer.
- **Clear Distribution Instructions**
  Outline how and when assets are

distributed—immediately, in stages, or upon specific conditions.

- **Provisions for Minors or Special Needs Beneficiaries**
  Include safeguards such as sub-trusts or guardianship provisions where appropriate.
- **Proper Execution**
  Ensure notarization and witnessing requirements are met according to local law.
- **Pour-Over Will Clause**
  Add a safety net for assets unintentionally left outside the trust.

Together, these elements form the backbone of a dependable living trust—one that protects your estate and carries out your wishes with precision.

The Battle Over Prince's Estate: Why Planning Matters

When iconic musician Prince died in 2016 without a will or trust, his estate—worth hundreds of millions—was left to the courts. Years of litigation followed, with assets tied up in legal proceedings and family disputes.

Prince's estate illustrates what happens when clarity is absent. Without named beneficiaries or instructions, decisions were made by default rather than design. The lesson is clear: estate planning is not about wealth—it's about control, protection, and peace of mind.

The Pour-Over Will: Completing the Picture

A pour-over will works alongside a living trust to ensure no asset is left behind. Its role is simple but vital:

1. **Captures Overlooked Assets**
   Any assets not transferred into the trust during your lifetime are directed into it upon death.
2. **Simplifies Administration**
   Consolidates asset management under one plan instead of splitting procedures.
3. **Preserves Privacy and Intent**
   Although the pour-over will passes through probate, it ultimately channels assets into the private trust structure.
4. **Acts as a Safety Net**
   Ensures your estate plan remains intact even if something is missed.

Together, the living trust and pour-over will create a seamless, comprehensive estate plan—one that leaves nothing to chance.

Choosing Your Trustee: The Naked Truth

A living trust is only as effective as the person—or institution—charged with carrying it out. That makes the trustee one of the most critical decisions in your entire estate plan.

The trustee is the steward of your trust: the individual who manages the assets, follows your instructions, and safeguards your beneficiaries' interests. It's a position of trust, accountability, and legal responsibility—not just a title.

Let's break it down clearly.

Trustee 101: Roles and Responsibilities

At its core, the trustee's job is to manage the trust assets responsibly and distribute them exactly as you've instructed. In practice, that role involves several key duties:

1. Asset Management

The trustee is responsible for managing trust assets prudently. This includes overseeing investments, preserving value, and making informed financial decisions that benefit the beneficiaries over time. The goal isn't speculation—it's stability, growth, and protection.

2. Distribution of Assets

Trustees distribute assets according to the terms you've set. That may mean paying for education, healthcare, living expenses, or releasing inheritances at specific ages or milestones. The trustee must follow your instructions precisely—no improvising.

3. Fiduciary Duty

A trustee is legally bound by fiduciary responsibility. This means they must always act in the best interests of the beneficiaries, avoid conflicts of interest, remain impartial, and never place personal gain above the trust's purpose.

4. Legal and Tax Compliance

Trust administration involves paperwork—sometimes a lot of it. Trustees must ensure compliance with state laws, file required tax returns, pay taxes owed, and keep detailed records of all trust activity.

5. Communication and Transparency

Good trustees communicate clearly and regularly. Beneficiaries should be informed about trust assets, distributions, and major decisions. Transparency prevents suspicion, conflict, and costly disputes.

In short: the trustee is the engine that keeps your trust running smoothly.

Selecting the Right Trustee for You

Choosing a trustee is a personal decision—but it should also be a practical one. Most people choose between an **individual trustee** and a **corporate trustee**, each with clear advantages and trade-offs.

Individual Trustees

Pros

- **Personal Connection**
  A family member or trusted friend often understands your values, family dynamics, and intentions on a deeper level.
- **Lower Cost**
  Individual trustees may charge minimal fees—or none at all—making this option more budget-friendly.

Cons

- **Limited Expertise**
  Managing investments, taxes, and legal compliance can be overwhelming for someone without professional experience.

- **Risk of Bias or Conflict**
  If the trustee is also a beneficiary, emotional decisions or perceived favoritism can create tension.

Corporate Trustees

Pros

- **Professional Expertise**
  Banks and trust companies bring financial, legal, and administrative experience to complex estates.
- **Continuity and Stability**
  Corporate trustees don't become incapacitated, pass away, or disengage. They operate under strict regulatory oversight.

Cons

- **Higher Costs**
  Fees are typically based on a percentage of the trust's assets and can add up over time.
- **Less Personal Touch**
  Institutions may lack familiarity with your family dynamics or personal wishes.

Making the Right Choice

When selecting a trustee, consider:

- The complexity of your estate
- The size of your trust assets
- Your budget for trustee fees
- Your need for professional oversight versus personal understanding

The right trustee is the one who best protects your beneficiaries and faithfully executes your plan—not necessarily the one who feels most familiar.

Understudies Matter: Naming Your Successor Trustees

Even the best trustee won't serve forever. That's why naming **successor trustees** is essential.

Successor trustees step in if the original trustee can no longer serve due to incapacity, resignation, or death—ensuring continuity and stability.

Key Considerations When Choosing Successor Trustees

- **Continuity**
  Successor trustees prevent disruptions and ensure your trust remains operational during transitions.
- **Trustworthiness and Capability**
  Choose individuals or institutions who understand your intentions, can act impartially, and are willing to serve.
- **Multiple Layers of Protection**
  Naming more than one successor—either sequentially or jointly—adds resilience. A mix of personal and professional trustees often works well.
- **Clear Documentation**
  Successor trustees must be clearly named in the trust document, along with conditions for assuming the role.
- **Ongoing Review**
  As relationships and circumstances change, revisit your selections to ensure they still make sense.

A well-planned succession ensures your trust never stalls when it matters most.

How to Fund Your Trust

Creating a trust without funding it is like buying a safe and never putting anything inside. Funding is what gives your trust power.

Which Assets Can—and Can't—Go Into a Trust

A living trust can hold a wide range of assets, including:

- Real estate
- Bank and brokerage accounts
- Stocks and bonds
- Business interests
- Personal property like art, jewelry, and vehicles

These assets are retitled in the name of the trust, allowing them to pass outside probate.

However, some assets require special handling:

- **Retirement accounts** (IRAs, 401(k)s) should generally not be retitled due to tax consequences.
- **Life insurance policies** typically name individuals as beneficiaries, though the trust may be named as beneficiary in some cases.

Proper coordination—not blind transfer—is key.

The Asset Transfer Process: Making It Official

Funding your trust means legally transferring ownership of assets into the trust's name.

This typically involves:

- Recording new deeds for real estate
- Retitling bank and investment accounts
- Updating ownership documents for vehicles and valuables

Meticulous record-keeping is essential. Assets not properly transferred may still pass through probate—defeating the purpose of the trust.

Professional guidance can help ensure transfers are done correctly and in compliance with state law.

Your Trust's Annual Check-Up: Manage, Review, Update

A living trust isn't a "set it and forget it" document. Life changes—and your trust should change with it.

Marriage, divorce, births, deaths, asset purchases, and sales all warrant a review.

Annual Trust Review Checklist

- Update your asset inventory
- Confirm all new assets are properly titled
- Reevaluate beneficiary designations

- Review trustee and successor trustee suitability
- Stay informed on legal and tax changes

Regular check-ups keep your trust aligned with your life and your goals.

Key Takeaways

- **Trustee selection is foundational** to effective trust administration
- **Both individual and corporate trustees** offer distinct advantages
- **Successor trustees ensure continuity and protection**
- **Proper funding is essential**—an unfunded trust won't work
- **Some assets require strategic coordination**, not direct transfer
- **Ongoing reviews keep your trust relevant and effective**

A living trust is a living plan—designed to grow, adapt, and protect across seasons of life.

Chapter 5

Understanding Taxes and Living Trusts

"In this world, nothing is certain except death and taxes."
— Benjamin Franklin

Estate Taxes and How Trusts Affect Them

If you're building a legacy, taxes are the silent guests you can't ignore. Estate, income, and gift taxes have a direct impact on how much of your hard-earned wealth actually reaches your heirs. The good news? With the right trust strategy, you can significantly reduce their bite.

This chapter explores how trusts interact with tax laws—and how smart planning can preserve more of your wealth for the people and causes you care about.

Untangling Estate Tax Laws and Your Trust

Understanding estate taxes is essential to effective estate planning. Estate tax—often referred to as the "death tax"—is assessed on the transfer of assets from a deceased person to their heirs. While the idea sounds straightforward, the way trusts interact with estate tax laws can dramatically change the outcome.

Federal Estate Tax Basics

The federal estate and gift tax applies **only to estates above a certain threshold**. For 2025, that exemption is:

- **$13.99 million per individual**
- **$27.98 million for married couples**

Estates below these limits owe no federal estate tax.

However, this window may not last.

Important Note:
Beginning in January 2026—unless Congress acts—the exemption is scheduled to revert to pre-2018 levels (adjusted for inflation). Current projections place the exemption at **approximately $7 million per individual**, though the final number will depend on inflation.

This potential reduction means individuals with sizable estates may benefit from taking action **before the higher exemption sunsets**, using gifts or trust-based strategies to lock in today's favorable limits.

Do Trusts Automatically Reduce Estate Taxes? (Short Answer: No)

A common misconception is that simply creating a trust eliminates estate taxes. That's not true—at least not with revocable living trusts.

Assets held in a **revocable living trust** are still considered part of your taxable estate because you retain control over them during your lifetime. From a tax perspective, nothing has changed.

That said, **certain types of trusts *can* reduce estate taxes when used strategically**.

Trusts That Can Reduce Estate Taxes

- **Irrevocable Trusts**
  Once assets are transferred into an irrevocable trust, they are no longer owned by the grantor. As a result, those assets are generally removed from the taxable estate.
- **Irrevocable Life Insurance Trusts (ILITs)**
  These trusts keep life insurance proceeds out of the taxable estate while still providing liquidity to heirs.
- **Charitable Trusts**
  Structures such as charitable remainder trusts or charitable lead trusts can reduce estate size while supporting philanthropic goals.

Leveraging Exemptions Through Strategic Gifting

Trusts can also help maximize the use of estate and gift tax exemptions:

- **Annual Gift Tax Exclusion**
  Assets can be gifted into certain trusts using the

annual exclusion, reducing estate size gradually without triggering gift tax.

- **Lifetime Exemption Planning**
  Larger transfers into irrevocable trusts can use a portion of the lifetime exemption to move appreciating assets out of the estate.
- **Marital Trust Strategies**
  Married couples can use structures like **AB trusts** (also called bypass trusts) to ensure both spouses' estate tax exemptions are fully utilized.

The key takeaway: **trusts don't eliminate estate taxes by default—but when structured intentionally, they can dramatically reduce them**.

How a Living Trust Can Be Kryptonite to Estate Taxes

When combined with the right strategies, trusts can neutralize much of the estate tax burden. Common approaches include:

- **Annual Gift Tax Exclusion Strategy**
  In 2025, individuals may gift up to **$19,000 per recipient** per year without gift tax. Married couples can double that amount. Funding an irrevocable trust with these gifts gradually shrinks the taxable estate.
- **Lifetime Exemption Transfers**
  Larger lump-sum transfers into irrevocable trusts can use lifetime exemptions strategically, removing future appreciation from the estate.
- **Generation-Skipping Transfer (GST) Trusts**
  These trusts pass assets directly to grandchildren or later generations, bypassing estate taxation at the

children's level (subject to GST rules and exemptions).

- **Charitable Lead Trusts (CLTs)**
  A CLT pays income to a charity for a fixed term, after which remaining assets pass to heirs—often with reduced or eliminated estate tax.
- **Life Insurance Trusts**
  An ILIT can own life insurance policies, keeping death benefits outside the taxable estate while providing tax-free liquidity.

Each of these strategies requires careful planning and professional guidance, but the payoff can be substantial.

Planning Ahead to Outsmart Future Estate Taxes

Tax laws change—but proactive planning keeps you ahead of them.

Smart estate planning isn't just about today's rules; it's about anticipating tomorrow's.

Forward-Thinking Strategies

- **Stay Informed**
  Work with professionals who monitor legislative changes and adjust strategies accordingly.
- **Build Flexibility into Trusts**
  Trust provisions can allow for adjustments based on future tax law changes.
- **Use Disclaimer Trusts**
  These give surviving spouses the option to fund trusts based on tax laws at the time of death—not assumptions made decades earlier.

- **Maximize Lifetime Gifting**
  Regular gifting reduces estate size and locks in current exemptions.
- **Diversify Assets**
  Different asset types are taxed differently—diversification creates planning options.
- **Consider Dynasty Trusts**
  For larger estates, dynasty trusts can preserve wealth across multiple generations while minimizing estate taxes over time.

Proactive planning today can prevent reactive—and expensive—decisions tomorrow.

A Lesson in Timing: George Steinbrenner's Estate

When New York Yankees owner **George Steinbrenner** passed away in 2010, federal estate taxes were temporarily repealed. His approximately **$1.1 billion estate** transferred to his heirs without the massive estate tax bill that would have applied in nearly any other year.

The result? **Hundreds of millions of dollars saved.**

Steinbrenner's case underscores a powerful truth: **timing, awareness, and preparedness matter**. While no one can predict legislative windows, staying informed and ready allows families to act decisively when opportunities arise.

Income Taxes: The Quiet Drain on Wealth

How Trusts Affect Your Income Taxes

Trusts don't just influence estate taxes—they also affect income taxation for both the trust and its beneficiaries. The impact depends largely on whether the trust is **revocable or irrevocable**.

Revocable Trusts and Income Taxes

For income tax purposes, revocable trusts are essentially invisible.

- Income generated by trust assets is taxed to the trustmaker
- The trustmaker reports income on their personal tax return
- The trust typically uses the trustmaker's Social Security number

In short, the IRS treats the assets as if they were never placed in a trust at all.

Irrevocable Trusts and Income Taxes

Irrevocable trusts are treated as **separate tax entities**.

- They require their own tax identification number
- They file their own tax returns
- Income retained in the trust is taxed at trust tax rates, which can be higher than individual rates

However, income distributed to beneficiaries is taxed at the beneficiaries' individual rates—often resulting in overall tax savings if beneficiaries fall into lower tax brackets.

Some irrevocable trusts, known as **grantor trusts**, intentionally shift income tax responsibility back to the grantor for strategic reasons.

Special and Emerging Tax Considerations

Trust taxation can be complex, especially with evolving policy proposals:

- Capital gains, interest, and dividends may be taxed differently depending on distribution timing
- Proposed changes for 2025 include treating certain transactions between grantors and grantor trusts as taxable events
- Another proposal suggests that paying a grantor trust's taxes could be treated as a taxable gift unless reimbursed

Trusts may also qualify for deductions related to administrative expenses and distributions, helping offset tax liability.

Bottom line: Trusts are powerful tax tools—but only when structured correctly and reviewed regularly. Strategic design and ongoing oversight can dramatically improve tax efficiency while staying compliant with the law.

The Trustee's Role in Managing Trust Income Taxes

A trustee's job doesn't stop at managing assets and making distributions. One of their most critical—and often overlooked—responsibilities is handling the trust's **income tax obligations**. This role demands diligence, organization, and a working understanding of tax rules to ensure compliance while preserving as much value as possible for beneficiaries.

Here's how trustees successfully manage trust income taxes:

Key Tax Responsibilities of a Trustee

Understanding the Trust's Tax Status

Not all trusts are taxed the same way. Trustees must clearly understand whether the trust is revocable or irrevocable, grantor or non-grantor, simple or complex—because each category carries different tax consequences. Misunderstanding this distinction can lead to costly mistakes.

Filing Annual Tax Returns

Trustees are responsible for filing the trust's annual income tax return using **IRS Form 1041**. This return reports income earned, deductions taken, and distributions made to beneficiaries. Accuracy and timeliness are essential.

Managing Distributions Strategically

Trustees often have discretion over when and how income is distributed. Since income distributed to beneficiaries is generally taxed at their personal income tax rates—often lower than trust tax rates—thoughtful distribution timing can reduce the overall tax burden.

Claiming Allowable Deductions

Administrative expenses, trustee fees, legal costs, and investment advisory fees may be deductible. Identifying and properly documenting these deductions can significantly reduce the trust's taxable income.

Communicating with Beneficiaries

Trustees must provide beneficiaries with **Schedule K-1 forms**, which detail the income distributed and the amount beneficiaries must report on their own tax returns. Clear communication helps prevent confusion and tax errors.

Working with Tax Professionals

Given the complexity of trust taxation, trustees often collaborate with CPAs or tax attorneys. Professional guidance ensures compliance, minimizes risk, and supports smart tax planning decisions.

Minimizing Trust Income Taxes

Reducing income taxes at the trust level requires foresight and intentional strategy. Trustees can use several proven techniques to protect trust assets and enhance long-term value for beneficiaries.

Practical Tax-Reduction Strategies

Strategic Income Distributions

Distributing income to beneficiaries in lower tax brackets can reduce overall taxes. This is especially effective for irrevocable trusts, which reach the highest tax brackets at much lower income levels than individuals.

Tax-Aware Investment Choices

Selecting investments with favorable tax characteristics—such as growth-oriented assets with minimal annual income—can defer taxes and reduce yearly taxable income. While this may involve greater market risk, it can be appropriate depending on the trust's goals.

Tax-Exempt Investments
Municipal bonds and other tax-exempt securities can generate income that is not subject to federal income tax, directly lowering the trust's tax exposure.

Charitable Distributions
If allowed under the trust document, making charitable distributions directly from the trust can reduce taxable income while fulfilling philanthropic objectives.

Maximizing Deductible Expenses
Careful documentation and full use of allowable deductions—such as trustee fees and professional expenses—can meaningfully reduce taxable income.

Trust Splitting (When Appropriate)
In some cases, dividing one trust into multiple trusts can optimize tax brackets and exemptions. This advanced strategy requires legal oversight to ensure compliance with tax laws.

Gift Taxes: Give and Plan Wisely

Understanding Gift Taxes in Trust Planning

Gift taxes apply when assets are transferred without receiving equal value in return. Trusts are commonly used for such transfers, making gift tax awareness essential in estate planning.

The IRS allows individuals to gift up to a certain amount each year to any individual without triggering gift tax or reducing their lifetime exemption. However, when gifts are made **to a trust**, qualification for this annual exclusion depends on whether beneficiaries receive a **present interest** in the gift.

To meet this requirement, many irrevocable trusts use **Crummey powers**, which give beneficiaries a limited window—often 30 days—to withdraw contributions. This temporary right converts the gift into a present interest, allowing it to qualify for the annual exclusion.

Gifts exceeding the annual exclusion typically count against the donor's **lifetime gift and estate tax exemption**. Transfers to irrevocable trusts are generally treated as completed gifts, making them powerful tools for removing appreciating assets from the taxable estate early.

If gifts exceed both the annual exclusion and remaining lifetime exemption, gift taxes may apply, and appropriate gift tax returns must be filed.

How Gifts Made Through a Trust Affect Taxes

Gifting from within a trust can be highly tax-efficient—but only if structured correctly.

- Gifts qualifying for the annual exclusion reduce estate size without triggering tax
- Crummey provisions are often necessary to qualify trust gifts for the exclusion
- Gifts exceeding exclusions reduce the donor's lifetime exemption
- Trustees must track cumulative gifts to avoid unintended tax consequences

Poor tracking or misunderstanding gift rules can lead to avoidable taxes and reporting issues.

Smart Gift-Giving Strategies Using Trusts

Trusts offer exceptional flexibility for transferring wealth efficiently. Common optimization strategies include:

- **Maximizing the Annual Gift Exclusion** through consistent, yearly trust contributions
- **Using Crummey Notices** to ensure gifts qualify for the exclusion
- **Applying Lifetime Exemptions Strategically** for larger transfers
- **Gifting Appreciating Assets** so future growth occurs outside the estate
- **Establishing GRATs** to transfer growth with minimal gift tax impact
- **Using Charitable Lead Trusts (CLTs)** to reduce gift and estate taxes while supporting causes
- **Maintaining Proper Documentation and Reporting** to remain compliant and preserve tax bencfits

A Real-World Example: Mark Zuckerberg's Gift Tax Strategy

Meta CEO **Mark Zuckerberg** and his wife, **Priscilla Chan**, demonstrate the power of early, strategic trust planning. By transferring Meta shares into a trust **before the company's IPO**, they leveraged lower valuations, maximizing the impact of their gift and estate tax exemptions.

This approach reduced future tax exposure while enabling large-scale philanthropy through the **Chan Zuckerberg Initiative**—a masterclass in combining charitable intent with tax efficiency.

Key Takeaways

- **Tax awareness is essential** to effective trust planning
- **Annual and lifetime exemptions** are powerful tools when used strategically
- **Trusts provide flexibility** for minimizing income, gift, and estate taxes
- **Timing matters**—early and informed decisions can save millions
- **Professional guidance is invaluable** in navigating complex tax rules
- **Adaptability ensures longevity**, allowing trusts to remain effective as laws and life circumstances evolve

Chapter 6

Updating Your Living Trust

"Change is the law of life. And those who look only to the past or present are certain to miss the future."
— John F. Kennedy

When Life Changes, Your Trust Should Too

A living trust is not a one-time document—it's a living plan that should evolve as your life evolves. As circumstances change, so should the instructions that guide how your assets are managed and distributed. Keeping your trust up to date ensures that it continues to reflect your current wishes, protects your loved ones, and complies with the law.

This chapter explains why regular reviews matter and highlights the key life events, financial changes, and legal developments that signal it's time to update your trust.

Updating Your Trust After Major Life Events

Life's milestones often bring joy, challenge, or both—and many of them require adjustments to your living trust. Events such as marriage, divorce, the birth of children, or the death of a loved one can significantly affect how you want your estate handled.

Marriage may prompt you to add your spouse as a beneficiary or appoint them as a co-trustee. Doing so requires a formal amendment to your trust to ensure their rights and responsibilities are clearly defined.

Divorce, on the other hand, often makes it necessary to remove a former spouse from the trust. Failing to do so can lead to unintended outcomes, including assets passing to someone you no longer wish to include.

Births and adoptions—whether of children or grandchildren—are another common reason to update a trust. You may want to add new beneficiaries, establish guardianship provisions, or set conditions on how and when assets are distributed, such as delaying inheritance until a beneficiary reaches a certain age or milestone.

Deaths of beneficiaries or trustees also require prompt attention. A deceased beneficiary's share may need to be redistributed, while the death of a trustee may require appointing a successor to prevent administrative delays or legal complications.

Beyond these immediate changes, major life events often reshape your broader estate planning goals. A growing family may call for more detailed instructions, additional sub-trusts, or provisions for education, healthcare, or long-term support.

Neglecting to update your trust after major life changes can create a gap between your current intentions and the legal reality of how your estate will be handled. This mismatch can lead to family disputes, court involvement, or outcomes you never intended. Reviewing your trust after each major event—and consulting an estate planning attorney when needed—helps keep your plan accurate and effective.

Why Births, Deaths, and Marriages Matter

Changes in family structure are among the most important triggers for revisiting your living trust. These moments reshape relationships, responsibilities, and priorities—and your estate plan should reflect that reality.

- **Births** introduce new potential beneficiaries. Updating your trust ensures that new children or grandchildren are included and properly provided for.
- **Deaths** can leave gaps in your plan. Whether it's a beneficiary or a trustee who passes away, your trust must be adjusted to reassign roles or redistribute assets smoothly.
- **Marriages**—your own or those of your beneficiaries—can change inheritance dynamics. You may wish to include a new spouse, consider protections against future divorces, or account for stepchildren.
- **Divorces** often require removing former spouses or adjusting distributions to protect your estate from unintended claims.

Each of these changes affects not only *who* benefits from your estate, but *how* and *when* those benefits are distributed.

A Real-World Example: Elizabeth Taylor

Actress and philanthropist Elizabeth Taylor experienced many personal changes throughout her life, including multiple marriages and a growing family. Rather than relying on a static plan, she consistently adjusted her trust to reflect her evolving circumstances.

Her carefully structured estate plan directed her substantial wealth to her children, grandchildren, and charitable causes she deeply valued. By updating her trust as her life changed, Taylor ensured that her wishes were honored and that her legacy was preserved with clarity and intention.

Adjusting Your Trust for Changes in Wealth

Financial circumstances rarely remain static. Whether your wealth grows or declines, your living trust should be updated to reflect your current reality and goals.

When wealth increases, new assets—such as investments, real estate, or business interests—should be formally transferred into your trust. You may also decide to expand your list of beneficiaries, increase distributions, or create structured timelines to help beneficiaries manage a larger inheritance responsibly.

When wealth decreases, it may be necessary to revise distribution amounts, prioritize certain beneficiaries, or adjust expectations to ensure fairness and sustainability.

Other important considerations include:

- **Updating trustee instructions** so asset management aligns with your current financial position.

- **Reviewing tax implications**, as changes in wealth can affect estate and income tax exposure.
- **Reevaluating distribution timing**, especially if staggered or conditional distributions would better protect beneficiaries.

All financial-based updates should be reviewed with an estate planning attorney or tax professional to ensure legal compliance and strategic alignment.

Case Insight: Steve Jobs

Steve Jobs was known for anticipating change—and that foresight extended to his estate planning. As Apple's valuation and his personal wealth grew, Jobs reportedly relied on trusts to manage and protect his assets.

While the details remain private, his approach highlights a key lesson: significant financial growth demands proactive estate planning adjustments. Revising a trust in response to wealth changes can help manage taxes, maintain privacy, and ensure assets are distributed according to your long-term vision.

Regular Reviews: Your Trust's Annual Check-Up

Just as regular medical check-ups help maintain good health, annual reviews help keep your living trust effective and relevant. A yearly review allows you to catch issues early and make thoughtful adjustments rather than rushed decisions later.

Regular trust reviews help you:

1. **Adapt to life changes** such as births, marriages, divorces, or deaths.
2. **Account for financial shifts** caused by investments, property transactions, or business changes.
3. **Respond to legal and tax updates** that may affect how your trust operates.
4. **Reevaluate trustees and beneficiaries** to ensure they still reflect your intentions.
5. **Clarify instructions** as your priorities and perspectives evolve over time.

An annual review doesn't always require changes—but it does ensure peace of mind, knowing your trust remains aligned with your life as it is today, not as it once was.

What to Look for in a Trust Review

A trust review is more than a quick glance at old paperwork. It's an opportunity to confirm that your living trust still reflects your intentions, protects your assets, and works smoothly under current laws. When reviewing your trust, focus on the following key areas:

Asset Listings:
This is the foundation of your trust review. Confirm that all assets intended to be held in the trust are properly titled and included. Update the list to reflect newly acquired assets or those that have been sold. For assets that have significantly increased or decreased in value, consider whether your original distribution plan still achieves balance and fairness among beneficiaries.

Beneficiary Designations:
Family dynamics evolve. Births, deaths, marriages, and divorces can all change who you want to benefit from your

trust. Review beneficiary designations carefully to ensure they align with your current wishes and relationships.

Trustee Arrangements:
Your trustee plays a central role in carrying out your trust's instructions. Reassess whether your current trustee and successor trustees are still the right choices, considering changes in their availability, health, location, or your level of trust in their judgment.

Distribution Plans:
Life circumstances change, and so do financial needs. Review how and when beneficiaries receive assets. You may want to adjust timing, conditions, or amounts to better reflect maturity levels, financial responsibility, or changing priorities.

Fiduciary and Tax Obligations:
Trust and tax laws evolve over time. Ensure your trust remains compliant and tax-efficient under current regulations. Staying informed in this area can help prevent unnecessary taxes and legal complications for your estate and beneficiaries.

Successor and Continuity Planning:
Finally, confirm that your trust includes clear instructions for succession if the current trustee can no longer serve. Proper planning ensures uninterrupted management and avoids confusion during critical transitions.

How to Conduct a Trust Review That Benefits You

A thoughtful trust review protects your assets and provides peace of mind. Follow this structured approach to ensure nothing is overlooked:

1. **Gather All Relevant Documents:**
   Collect the original trust agreement, amendments, asset inventories, and records of prior reviews.
2. **Review Trustee and Successor Trustee Appointments:**
   Confirm that the individuals named are still appropriate and capable of fulfilling their responsibilities.
3. **Assess Asset Titles and Listings:**
   Verify that all trust assets are properly titled and that new or sold assets are accurately reflected.
4. **Examine Beneficiary Designations:**
   Ensure beneficiary details reflect current family relationships and intentions.
5. **Evaluate Distribution Provisions:**
   Review whether distribution terms still make sense given beneficiaries' ages, needs, and circumstances.
6. **Consult with Professionals:**
   Discuss your findings with an estate planning attorney or financial advisor to identify needed adjustments and legal considerations.
7. **Document and Implement Changes:**
   Any updates should be formally drafted, executed, and properly recorded to avoid ambiguity.
8. **Communicate Important Updates:**
   Inform trustees, successor trustees, and relevant beneficiaries about significant changes to ensure clarity and prevent misunderstandings.

Amending vs. Restating: Understanding Trust Updates

Keeping a living trust current requires knowing when to amend it and when a full restatement is the better option.

Amendments:
An amendment makes targeted changes to an existing trust without rewriting the entire document. It's ideal for minor updates, such as changing a trustee, updating a beneficiary's name, or adjusting a specific provision. Amendments are typically drafted as separate documents and attached to the original trust.

Restatements:
A restatement replaces the entire trust document while keeping the original trust name and date intact. This option is best when multiple changes are needed or when previous amendments have made the trust confusing. A restatement consolidates all updates into a single, clear document.

When to Amend and When to Restate

Amendments are well-suited for small, straightforward changes that don't affect the trust's overall structure. However, when changes are substantial—such as reorganizing distributions, revising beneficiary structures, or simplifying a heavily amended trust—a restatement offers clarity and efficiency.

The Update Process

Amending a Trust:
An amendment document specifies the exact changes, references the original trust, and is signed and notarized according to legal requirements.

Restating a Trust:
A restated trust is a newly written agreement that replaces all prior versions. It must clearly state that it supersedes earlier documents and be signed and notarized to be legally valid.

In both cases, working with an estate planning attorney is strongly advised to ensure the updates are legally sound and aligned with your goals.

Key Takeaways

- **Stay Proactive:** Regular updates keep your trust aligned with your life and intentions.
- **Family Changes Matter:** Births, deaths, marriages, and divorces often require trust revisions.
- **Wealth Shifts Require Attention:** Significant financial changes should prompt a review.
- **Annual Reviews Are Essential:** A yearly check-up helps catch issues early.
- **Amend vs. Restate Wisely:** Choose the approach that best matches the scope of changes.
- **Professional Guidance Protects Your Legacy:** Expert advice ensures clarity, compliance, and long-term effectiveness.

Chapter 7

Risks, Limitations & Drawbacks

"In preparing for battle, I have always found that plans are useless, but planning is indispensable."— Dwight D. Eisenhower, 34th President of the United States

What Living Trusts Can and Cannot Do

Living trusts are powerful estate planning tools, but they are not magic solutions. Understanding both their strengths *and* their limitations is essential to using them effectively. This chapter provides a clear-eyed look at what trusts can't do, the risks of poor planning, the hidden costs involved, and practical ways to reduce potential drawbacks—so you can protect your assets and your family with clarity and confidence.

Due Diligence Alert: Trusts Have Limits Too

Trusts offer flexibility, privacy, and control, but they are still governed by law and reality. Recognizing these limits helps set realistic expectations and prevents costly surprises.

First, **trusts are subject to legal authority**. While they may offer a degree of protection, they cannot fully shield assets from certain obligations. Claims related to taxes, child support, alimony, or court judgments may still reach trust assets—especially if the trust was created to evade creditors.

Second, **a trust is only as effective as its funding and administration**. A beautifully drafted trust accomplishes little if assets are not properly transferred into it. Any asset left outside the trust may still be subject to probate, undermining one of the trust's main advantages.

Third, **trusts do not eliminate all taxes**. While some trust structures can reduce estate or income taxes, others—particularly revocable living trusts—offer no estate tax reduction at all. Their primary benefit lies in control and probate avoidance, not tax elimination.

Finally, **trusts cannot prevent family conflict**. While they can clearly define asset distribution, they cannot stop disputes, resentment, or legal challenges from unhappy heirs. Clear drafting and open communication can reduce conflict, but they cannot guarantee harmony.

Trusts are highly effective when used correctly—but understanding their boundaries is essential to using them wisely.

Why Trusts Can't Shield You from All Creditors

A common misconception is that placing assets in a trust makes them untouchable. In reality, several categories of creditors can still access trust assets under certain circumstances:

- **Secured Debts:** If trust-owned property secures a loan (such as a mortgage), the lender can still enforce its rights if payments are not made.
- **Federal Tax Liabilities:** The IRS has broad authority to collect unpaid taxes and may reach trust assets when legally permitted.
- **State Tax Obligations:** State tax agencies may also claim trust assets to satisfy unpaid state taxes.
- **Child Support and Alimony:** Courts prioritize these obligations, and trust assets may be used if other resources are insufficient.
- **Court Judgments:** Certain legal judgments—such as personal injury awards—may allow creditors access to trust assets, depending on timing and trust type.
- **Fraudulent Transfers:** Assets placed into a trust to deliberately avoid creditors can be clawed back by the courts.

Trusts provide structure and planning advantages, but they must be designed with a realistic understanding of creditor laws.

When a Trust Can't Bypass Probate

Although avoiding probate is a primary reason many people establish living trusts, probate avoidance is not automatic. Common situations where probate may still occur include:

- **Improperly Funded Trusts:** Assets not formally transferred into the trust remain part of the probate estate.
- **Overlooked or Minor Assets:** Small accounts, personal property, or newly acquired assets not added to the trust may still require probate.
- **Out-of-State Real Estate:** Property owned in another state may trigger ancillary probate unless specifically addressed within the trust.

Practical Steps to Reduce Probate Exposure

1. **Conduct a Full Asset Review:** Ensure all assets are properly titled in the trust's name and update the list regularly.
2. **Use a Pour-Over Will:** This acts as a backup, transferring any overlooked assets into the trust after death (though probate may still be required).
3. **Plan for Multi-State Property:** Transfer out-of-state real estate into the trust or use specialized planning strategies.
4. **Review the Trust Regularly:** Life changes and new assets require updates to keep the trust effective.

Common Mistakes and Poor Planning Pitfalls

The Risks of DIY Trusts: Why YouTube Isn't Enough

Online templates and videos make trust creation look easy—but estate planning is rarely one-size-fits-all. DIY trusts often introduce serious risks:

Common Problems with Self-Made Trusts

- **Legal Errors:** Trust laws vary by state, and generic documents may not comply with local requirements.
- **Missed Complexities:** Family dynamics, blended families, special-needs beneficiaries, and business assets require tailored planning.
- **Drafting Mistakes:** Errors in language or coordination with other estate documents can lead to disputes or unintended disinheritance.

Why Professional Guidance Matters

- Customized planning that reflects your unique goals
- Compliance with current state laws
- Integration with wills, powers of attorney, and tax strategies
- Ongoing support as laws and life circumstances change

While DIY options may save money upfront, they often create far greater financial and emotional costs later.

Consequences of Overlooking Successor Trustees

A successor trustee ensures continuity when the original trustee can no longer serve. Failing to plan carefully for this role can disrupt the entire trust.

Role of a Successor Trustee

- Managing trust assets
- Filing taxes and maintaining records
- Making distributions to beneficiaries
- Acting with fiduciary responsibility and legal accountability

Risks of Poor Succession Planning

- **Administrative Delays:** Asset distribution may stall if no successor is clearly named.
- **Family Disputes:** Uncertainty can lead to conflict or court involvement.
- **Higher Costs:** Court-appointed trustees and legal disputes increase expenses.
- **Compromised Intent:** Your wishes may not be carried out as intended.

Best Practices

- Choose someone capable, trustworthy, and willing
- Consider professional or institutional trustees for complex estates
- Provide clear written guidance within the trust document

Understanding The Real Cost of Living Trusts

Understanding the Financial Commitment

Trusts offer powerful benefits, but they are not free.

Initial Costs May Include

- Attorney fees for drafting
- Asset retitling and funding costs
- Financial planning or advisory fees

Ongoing Costs May Include

- Trustee fees (especially professional trustees)
- Legal consultations
- Tax preparation and filing fees
- Investment management costs

Weighing Costs Against Benefits

Despite these expenses, trusts often deliver substantial long-term value—greater control, privacy, tax efficiency, and probate avoidance. For many estates, these benefits outweigh the financial commitment.

A Cautionary Example: James Gandolfini's Estate

Actor James Gandolfini passed away in 2013 with an estate valued at roughly $70 million. Although he had an estate plan, the structure resulted in an estimated $30 million in estate taxes—much of which could potentially have been reduced through more strategic trust planning.

His case highlights an important truth: **having an estate plan is not enough—how it's structured matters.** Trusts must be designed and implemented thoughtfully to preserve wealth and protect beneficiaries.

Legal Fees, Taxes, and Other Hidden Trust Expenses

While living trusts offer powerful benefits, they are not free from ongoing costs. Beyond the initial setup and routine maintenance, trustees and beneficiaries may encounter legal fees, taxes, and other expenses that are not always obvious at first glance. Left unmanaged, these costs can quietly erode the value of the trust over time. Understanding them—and planning ahead—helps ensure the trust fulfills its purpose without unnecessary financial drain.

Common Trust-Related Expenses

Legal Fees

Trusts often require periodic legal guidance, especially when updates, amendments, or disputes arise. Changes in family circumstances, tax laws, or asset structures may necessitate professional review. Legal costs vary widely depending on complexity and the expertise of the attorney involved, but they are an ongoing consideration in long-term trust management.

Taxes

Trusts file their own tax returns and are subject to unique tax rules. In many cases, trusts reach higher tax brackets more quickly than individuals. The tax treatment depends heavily on the type of trust. Revocable trusts typically pass income tax responsibility to the grantor, while irrevocable trusts may offer tax advantages—but at the cost of reduced control over the assets.

Other Less-Visible Expenses

Additional costs may include asset appraisals, investment management fees, insurance premiums, and administrative services. Trusts that hold real estate can also incur property taxes, maintenance expenses, and insurance costs. These expenses may seem minor individually, but over time, they add up.

Five Practical Strategies to Control Trust Expenses

1. **Conduct Annual Reviews**
   Regular check-ins with legal and financial professionals can help identify inefficiencies, eliminate unnecessary fees, and ensure the trust remains aligned with its goals.
2. **Prioritize Smart Tax Planning**
   A knowledgeable tax professional can help structure distributions, charitable giving, and income strategies to reduce tax exposure while staying compliant.
3. **Evaluate Corporate Trustees Carefully**
   For complex or high-value trusts, a corporate trustee may offer professional oversight and administrative efficiency. While they charge fees, their experience can sometimes prevent costly mistakes or disputes.
4. **Maintain Transparent Communication**
   Clear and open communication among trustees and beneficiaries reduces misunderstandings that often lead to expensive legal conflicts.
5. **Review Investment Strategies Regularly**
   Ensure the trust's investments match its objectives and risk tolerance. Poor investment choices or excessive management fees can undermine long-term growth.

The Emotional Cost: Navigating Family Dynamics

Trust administration is not purely financial—it is deeply personal. Trusts often bring underlying family tensions to the surface, particularly when decisions involve asset distribution, trustee appointments, or delayed inheritances. These emotional dynamics can strain relationships long after the trust is established.

Perceived favoritism, unequal distributions, or misunderstandings about trustee authority can foster resentment and mistrust. When a family member serves as trustee, beneficiaries may question decisions—even when they are appropriate and lawful. Additionally, creating a trust forces families to confront difficult topics such as mortality, inheritance, and legacy—conversations many prefer to avoid.

Reducing Emotional Strain

- **Open Communication**
  Clearly explain the trust's purpose and reasoning behind key decisions to help manage expectations.
- **Inclusive Discussions**
  When appropriate, involving beneficiaries in conversations can promote understanding and a sense of fairness.
- **Professional Mediation**
  A neutral third party can help guide emotionally charged discussions and prevent conflict from escalating.
- **Clear Documentation**
  Well-drafted trust documents that reflect the grantor's intent leave less room for misinterpretation.
- **Education**
  Helping beneficiaries understand how trusts

work—and what trustees are legally required to do—can reduce suspicion and resentment.

- **Regular Reviews**
  Revisiting the trust periodically allows adjustments as family circumstances evolve.

Case Insight: Robin Williams and the Power of Privacy

When beloved actor and comedian Robin Williams passed away in 2014, his estate plan demonstrated the strength of thoughtful trust planning. Williams created trusts for his children that distributed benefits gradually rather than as a single lump sum. This structure offered financial protection while supporting them at different life stages.

Importantly, his use of trusts kept estate details private and largely out of the public eye—avoiding the exposure that often accompanies probate proceedings. While disputes did arise between his widow and children from previous marriages, the clarity and foresight built into his trust documents helped resolve matters more efficiently and discreetly than would otherwise have been possible.

Williams' estate highlights how a well-designed trust can protect privacy, manage family dynamics, and preserve dignity during an emotionally difficult time.

Key Takeaways

- **Trusts Have Limits**
  Trusts offer flexibility and protection, but they cannot eliminate all taxes, creditor claims, or legal challenges.

- **Funding Is Critical**
  A trust must be properly funded to work. Unfunded assets may still go through probate.
- **DIY Comes With Risks**
  Creating a trust without professional guidance can result in costly legal and financial mistakes.
- **Trustee Selection Matters**
  Choosing the right successor trustee is essential for smooth administration and family harmony.
- **Hidden Costs Exist**
  Legal fees, taxes, and investment expenses require ongoing attention to prevent erosion of trust assets.
- **Emotions Are Part of the Equation**
  Trusts affect families, not just finances. Proactive communication and planning help protect relationships as well as assets.

Chapter 8

How Living Trusts Impact Beneficiaries

"The greatest use of a life is to spend it on something that will outlast it."— William James

Inheritance Timing: A Matter of Trust

Living trusts do more than transfer assets—they shape the financial future of the people you leave behind. For beneficiaries, understanding **when**, **how**, and **under what conditions** they receive an inheritance is just as important as the inheritance itself.

This chapter explores how living trusts affect beneficiaries, including inheritance timing, tax implications, and the role—and limits—of trustees.

When and How Beneficiaries Receive Their Inheritance

One of the primary advantages of a living trust is its ability to provide structure, clarity, and control over asset distribution. Unlike a will, which only becomes effective after death, a living trust can operate during the grantor's lifetime, upon incapacity, or after death—depending on how it's designed.

How Asset Distribution Works

A living trust becomes effective as soon as it is created and properly funded. The grantor establishes the rules for how assets are managed and distributed, and appoints a trustee to carry out those instructions. The trustee is legally obligated to follow the trust's terms and act in the best interests of the beneficiaries.

This flexibility allows assets to be distributed:

- During the grantor's lifetime
- If the grantor becomes incapacitated
- After the grantor's death

Each option offers different benefits depending on the grantor's goals.

What Can Affect the Timing of Inheritance

Even with a well-structured trust, distributions are rarely instantaneous. Several factors can influence how quickly beneficiaries receive assets:

Conditions Set by the Grantor
The grantor may require beneficiaries to meet specific conditions—such as reaching a certain age, completing

education, or achieving personal milestones—before receiving distributions.

Type of Asset
Some assets, including real estate or business interests, require additional legal or financial steps to transfer. These complexities can slow distribution.

Trustee Responsibilities
Before distributing assets, trustees must ensure that all debts, taxes, and administrative obligations are settled. The trustee's efficiency and workload can affect timelines.

Legal or Family Disputes
Challenges from beneficiaries or other family members can temporarily halt distributions until disputes are resolved.

State Laws
While trusts typically avoid probate, certain state laws may still influence timing or procedural requirements.

Understanding these factors helps beneficiaries form realistic expectations and highlights the importance of thoughtful trust design.

Why Distributions May Be Delayed—Even With a Trust

Although living trusts are designed to streamline inheritance, delays can still occur. Common reasons include:

1. **Complex Distribution Rules**
   Detailed or conditional instructions may require time to satisfy.

2. **Illiquid Assets**
   Assets that can't be quickly sold or transferred—such as property or private businesses—often delay payouts.

3. **Beneficiary Disputes**
   Conflicts over trust terms or asset management can trigger legal intervention.

4. **Improper Funding**
   Assets not correctly titled to the trust may still need to pass through probate or other legal processes.

5. **Outstanding Taxes or Debts**
   Trustees must resolve financial obligations before making distributions.

While delays can be frustrating, they are often necessary to protect the integrity of the trust and ensure compliance with the grantor's intentions.

Tax Considerations for Beneficiaries

How Trusts Affect Beneficiary Taxes

Taxes are one of the most misunderstood aspects of trust inheritance. The impact on beneficiaries depends on the trust's structure and how distributions are handled.

Type of Trust
Revocable trusts generally pass income tax responsibility to the grantor during their lifetime. Irrevocable trusts, however, are separate tax entities and follow different rules.

Distributable Net Income (DNI)
Beneficiaries are typically taxed on income distributed to them, such as interest, dividends, or rental income, at their personal tax rates.

Principal Distributions
Distributions of the original trust assets are usually not subject to income tax. However, capital gains tax may apply if assets have appreciated and are sold.

Undistributed Income
If income is retained within the trust, the trust itself pays taxes—often at higher rates than individuals.

Timing Matters
Trusts may elect to treat distributions made early in the following year as if they occurred in the prior tax year, affecting tax planning for beneficiaries.

State Taxes
State tax laws vary widely and can significantly influence a beneficiary's overall tax burden.

Because trust taxation is complex, beneficiaries should work closely with tax professionals to avoid surprises.

Case Insight: The Walton Family Trusts

The Walton family—heirs to the Walmart fortune—have long relied on a sophisticated network of trusts to manage, protect, and transfer wealth across generations. Their strategic use of trusts demonstrates how careful planning can preserve wealth, reduce tax exposure, and align financial decisions with long-term family values.

By using different trust structures for different purposes, the Waltons have ensured continuity, minimized tax liabilities, and maintained control over how their legacy unfolds. Their approach highlights the power of proactive trust planning at any scale.

Inheritance Tax vs. Income Tax: What Beneficiaries Must Know

Beneficiaries should clearly understand the difference between these two taxes:

Inheritance Tax
Some states impose an inheritance tax on beneficiaries who receive assets. Rates depend on state law and the beneficiary's relationship to the deceased. Many states impose no inheritance tax at all.

Income Tax
Income generated by trust assets—such as interest or dividends—is taxable to beneficiaries when distributed. Any income retained by the trust is taxed at the trust level.

Knowing which taxes apply helps beneficiaries plan wisely and avoid unnecessary financial stress.

Case Study: The Battle Over B.B. King's Estate

When legendary blues musician **B.B. King** passed away in 2015, he left behind an extraordinary musical legacy—but also an estate plan that became the subject of intense legal dispute. Despite efforts at estate planning, the absence of a clearly structured and well-communicated trust resulted in conflicting claims among family members and associates.

The disagreements surrounding King's estate underscored how even substantial wealth and good intentions can unravel when estate documents lack precision. Ambiguities in planning opened the door to legal challenges, prolonged court proceedings, and emotional strain among those left behind.

The battle over B.B. King's estate serves as a powerful reminder: **estate planning is not merely about having documents in place, but about ensuring those documents are thorough, unambiguous, and clearly communicated to all involved parties.** A carefully drafted trust can mean the difference between a smooth transition of legacy and years of conflict.

Key Takeaways

Understanding Inheritance Mechanics
Beneficiaries should have a clear understanding of how and when assets are distributed through a living trust. While trusts often allow for faster and more private distributions than probate, delays can still occur due to trust terms, asset types, or disputes.

Tax Awareness Is Essential
Beneficiaries must understand the tax implications of trust distributions, particularly the difference between inheritance tax and income tax. This knowledge is critical for effective financial planning and avoiding unexpected tax liabilities.

Trustee Authority Has Limits
Although trustees are granted significant control over trust assets, their authority is constrained by fiduciary duties, the trust document itself, state law, and the legal rights of beneficiaries.

Beneficiaries Have the Right to Challenge
Beneficiaries are not powerless. They may challenge a trustee's actions in cases of fiduciary breaches,

mismanagement, excessive fees, failure to communicate, or deviations from the trust's terms.

Professional Guidance Matters

Given the legal, financial, and emotional complexities involved in trust administration, beneficiaries are strongly advised to seek guidance from qualified estate planning attorneys and tax professionals. Expert advice can help protect both the inheritance and family relationships.

Chapter 9

Living Trusts In The Modern World

"The only real security that a man can have in this world is a reserve of knowledge, experience, and ability."
— Henry Ford, founder of Ford Motor Company

Trusts in the Digital Age

In today's world, our lives exist as much online as they do offline. As a result, protecting digital assets has become an essential part of modern estate planning. While trusts have long been used to manage tangible wealth, they now play a vital role in securing our digital presence and online legacies.

Protecting Digital and Online Accounts

With so much of our personal and professional lives stored digitally—from email accounts and social media profiles to digital wallets and online businesses—it's crucial to account for these assets when planning your estate. The first step is to create a detailed inventory of your digital holdings, including access information such as usernames, passwords, and clear instructions for their management and distribution.

However, managing digital assets is more complex than managing physical property. Terms of service agreements from various platforms can impact whether and how accounts or assets can be transferred after death. For this reason, consulting with an estate planning attorney experienced in digital assets is essential. They can help you structure your trust to include these digital possessions properly, ensuring smooth, lawful transfer while protecting your privacy.

Because digital assets often evolve rapidly, regular updates to your estate plan are crucial. Annual reviews help capture new assets or changes to existing ones, keeping your plan current with your digital life.

Protecting Your Digital Music and eBooks

Including digital music and eBook collections in a trust requires careful navigation of unique legal challenges and specific strategies to ensure these intangible assets are preserved for beneficiaries. Key considerations include:

- **Understanding Licensing Agreements:** Most digital content is purchased under licenses that often restrict transfer or inheritance. Reviewing the terms of service for each platform is essential to determine what's legally permitted regarding digital music and eBook transfers.
- **Cataloging Your Collections:** Create a detailed inventory of your digital music and eBooks, noting

where they are stored and any relevant account access information.

- **Clear Trust Instructions:** Specify how these assets should be managed within the trust. This might include granting access to certain individuals, instructions to repurchase content if transfers aren't allowed, or allocating funds for beneficiaries to obtain these assets legally.
- **Choosing the Right Trustee:** Appoint a trustee familiar with digital asset management and who appreciates the value of your collections.
- **Consider a Digital Executor:** For complex digital portfolios, a dedicated digital executor can work alongside the trustee to ensure proper handling of digital music and eBooks.

Privacy, Technology and Your Estate

The intersection of trusts and data privacy laws adds a layer of complexity to managing digital assets. Trusts must operate within strict legal frameworks designed to protect personal information, considering:

- **Data Privacy Laws:** Regulations like the EU's GDPR and U.S. state laws such as the California Consumer Privacy Act (CCPA) impose stringent rules on handling personal data. These affect how trustees access and distribute digital assets containing sensitive information.
- **Consent and Access:** Many laws require explicit consent to transfer personal data, complicating trustees' access to accounts like email and social media. Trusts need clear provisions granting this consent or lawful authority.
- **Legal Authority vs. Service Agreements:** Even with a trust, service providers' terms of use may

limit asset transfer after death. Trustees must navigate these terms while complying with privacy laws, often requiring legal guidance.

- **Protecting Beneficiaries' Privacy:** Trustees must safeguard beneficiaries' personal information in line with the trust's terms and applicable privacy regulations.

Managing digital assets within the bounds of privacy laws demands careful coordination to protect both the trustmaker's and beneficiaries' information.

Trusts as Shields: Your Digital Privacy's Secret Weapon

Trusts offer a powerful tool for protecting your digital privacy by providing:

- **Anonymity:** Holding assets in a trust's name, rather than personally, adds a layer of privacy—valuable for individuals concerned about security and discretion.
- **Controlled Access:** Trustees' powers and responsibilities are clearly defined, ensuring only authorized persons can manage sensitive digital information.
- **Legal Protections:** Trusts offer a legal framework that safeguards digital assets from risks like hacking and identity theft through formal management standards.
- **Succession Planning:** Trusts enable seamless, private transfer of digital assets upon death or incapacity, respecting the trustmaker's wishes and maintaining confidentiality.
- **Compliance with Privacy Laws:** Trusts can be structured to meet data privacy requirements,

reducing the risk of legal complications related to personal data.

The Limits of Trusts in Protecting Online Privacy

Despite their strengths, trusts face several challenges when it comes to digital privacy:

- **Jurisdictional Complexities:** Digital assets often span multiple countries with differing laws, making trust enforcement across borders difficult.
- **Terms of Service Restrictions:** Many platforms restrict account transfer or management after death, sometimes overriding trust provisions.
- **Technological Barriers:** Encryption and security measures may impede trustees' access, especially without technical expertise or legal authority.
- **Rapidly Evolving Digital Landscape:** New types of digital assets and technologies emerge constantly, requiring ongoing trust updates to remain effective.
- **Balancing Privacy and Access:** Trustees need sufficient access to manage assets without compromising sensitive information, a delicate and ongoing challenge.

These limitations underscore the importance of combining legal, technical, and practical approaches to effectively protect digital assets and privacy.

Key Takeaways

- **Comprehensive Inclusion:** Incorporating all digital assets—social media, cryptocurrency, digital business assets—into trusts is essential in today's estate planning.

- **Legal Navigation:** Successful digital asset management demands careful attention to data privacy laws and platform agreements.
- **Privacy Protection:** Trusts offer anonymity and controlled access, shielding sensitive digital information from unauthorized exposure.
- **Regular Reviews:** The fast-changing digital world makes frequent updates to your trust necessary to keep pace with new assets and technologies.
- **Challenges Remain:** Jurisdictional conflicts, service terms, and technical obstacles present ongoing hurdles in digital estate management.
- **Future-Proofing:** Effective digital asset planning anticipates future developments, ensuring assets remain protected and privacy is upheld over time.

Chapter 10

What Happens After Death?

"To listen well is as powerful a means of communication and influence as to talk well." — John Marshall, Fourth Chief Justice of the United States

How Trust Administration Works

The death of a trustor marks the beginning of the trust administration process, a crucial period that can often feel complex and overwhelming. Proper preparation, combined with clear and timely communication, is essential to ensure the trust is administered smoothly and in accordance with the trustor's wishes. This chapter aims to demystify this process by outlining the key steps and responsibilities trustees and beneficiaries will encounter during this transition.

The Importance of Keeping Beneficiaries Informed Before Death

One of the most effective ways to prevent confusion, conflict, and delays after a trustor's passing is to maintain open communication with beneficiaries well in advance. By sharing relevant information about the trust and its intentions, trustors provide clarity and reassurance. The advantages of early communication include:

- **Reducing Uncertainty and Preventing Conflict:** When beneficiaries understand what assets are in the trust and the reasons behind specific distribution decisions, there is less room for misunderstandings or disputes that can otherwise lead to costly and prolonged legal battles.
- **Enabling Beneficiaries to Plan Ahead:** Awareness of anticipated inheritances allows beneficiaries to make informed financial decisions, whether related to personal budgeting, investments, or major life choices such as purchasing property, pursuing education, or career planning.
- **Fostering Trust and Cooperation:** Introducing beneficiaries to trustees and explaining their roles can build a cooperative relationship based on respect and understanding. This rapport is invaluable during the administration process, which can involve sensitive decisions.
- **Easing Emotional Burdens:** The period following a loved one's death is naturally emotional and stressful. When beneficiaries know what to expect regarding asset distribution and trust management, some of that stress is alleviated, allowing them to focus on healing and moving forward.
- **Promoting Transparency and Accountability:** Open dialogue demonstrates the trustor's commitment to honesty and fairness, which reinforces confidence in the trustee's administration of the trust and helps maintain family harmony.

Through early and clear communication, trustors not only protect their estate but also nurture enduring family relationships.

A Step-by-Step Guide to Trust Administration

Understanding the phases of trust administration can help trustees and beneficiaries navigate the process with confidence and clarity. Each step has distinct goals and responsibilities that collectively ensure the trust's proper execution:

1. **Notification of Beneficiaries:**
   The first official task for the trustee is to notify all named beneficiaries that the trust exists and that administration will begin. This formal communication initiates transparency and sets expectations about the timeline and procedures ahead. Trustees may also explain their role and provide an overview of what beneficiaries can expect.
2. **Inventory and Appraisal of Assets:**
   Trustees must compile a thorough inventory of all assets held within the trust. This inventory may include real estate, investments, bank accounts, personal property, and digital assets. For many assets, professional appraisals or valuations are necessary to establish their fair market value, which is critical for accurate accounting, tax filings, and equitable distribution.
3. **Payment of Debts and Taxes:**
   Before beneficiaries receive any distributions, the trustee is responsible for identifying and settling the trustor's outstanding debts, such as mortgages, loans, or credit card balances. Additionally, any applicable estate, income, or inheritance taxes must

be calculated and paid. Fulfilling these obligations helps prevent legal issues that could jeopardize the trust's assets or delay distribution.

4. **Management and Investment of Trust Assets:** Throughout the administration period, trustees often need to manage or invest trust assets prudently. This includes maintaining real estate, managing investment portfolios, or overseeing business interests. Trustees must act according to the trust's terms and exercise fiduciary care, always prioritizing the beneficiaries' best interests.
5. **Distribution of Assets to Beneficiaries:** Once debts and taxes are settled and assets are appropriately managed, trustees begin distributing assets as specified in the trust agreement. Distributions may be outright or staggered over time, depending on the trust's instructions. Trustees must follow these directions carefully and keep detailed records of all distributions made.
6. **Final Accounting and Closure:** At the conclusion of the administration process, the trustee prepares a comprehensive final accounting for beneficiaries. This report details all financial activities, including asset management, income received, expenses paid, taxes settled, and distributions made. Upon approval of this accounting by the beneficiaries or court (if required), the trustee formally closes the trust, marking the end of their duties.

Next Steps: Immediate Actions Following a Trustor's Death

To ensure the trust administration process starts off on the right foot, certain critical actions should be taken immediately after the trustor's passing:

- **Obtain Multiple Death Certificates:** These are essential for proving the trustor's death to financial institutions, government agencies, and other entities involved in transferring assets.
- **Notify Beneficiaries and Relevant Institutions:** Trustees should inform all beneficiaries and any financial institutions, investment firms, or custodians holding trust assets about the trustor's passing and the activation of the trust.
- **Secure Trust Assets:** It's vital to protect trust assets by securing physical properties, updating security measures, and safeguarding digital assets to prevent loss or theft during administration.
- **Review Trust Documents Thoroughly:** The trustee must carefully examine the trust document to understand their responsibilities, asset distribution plans, and any special instructions or conditions.
- **Engage Legal and Financial Professionals:** Trustees should seek guidance from estate attorneys, accountants, or financial advisors to ensure compliance with legal requirements and proper administration.
- **Begin Asset Inventory:** Starting a detailed inventory of trust assets early helps streamline subsequent appraisal, management, and distribution efforts.

Your Secret Weapon Against Probate Costs

Minimizing or eliminating probate expenses requires thoughtful trust planning and diligent administration. By taking strategic steps, you can protect your assets and ensure they transfer efficiently to your beneficiaries.

Consider these key strategies as your safeguard against unnecessary probate costs:

- **Comprehensive Trust Funding:** Make sure all significant assets are properly placed into the trust. Fully funding the trust helps avoid probate for those assets, allowing a quicker and more private transfer to beneficiaries.
- **Regular Asset Reviews and Trust Updates:** Periodically review your asset portfolio alongside your trust documents. This ensures that new acquisitions or financial changes are captured and incorporated into the trust, maintaining protection against probate.
- **Utilize Transfer-on-Death (TOD) and Payable-on-Death (POD) Designations:** For accounts such as retirement funds and life insurance policies, TOD and POD designations allow direct transfers to beneficiaries without probate involvement.
- **Joint Ownership with Right of Survivorship:** Holding property or accounts jointly with a spouse or trusted individual can automatically transfer ownership upon death, bypassing probate.
- **Lifetime Gifting:** Transferring assets as gifts during your lifetime can reduce the probate estate size. However, keep in mind annual gift tax exclusions to optimize tax advantages.
- **Work with Estate Planning Professionals:** Collaborate with attorneys and financial advisors who specialize in estate planning. Their expertise can help customize strategies that minimize probate costs while maximizing tax benefits and asset protection.

By implementing these measures, you can significantly reduce probate expenses, preserving more of your estate for your loved ones.

The Case of Philip Seymour Hoffman's Estate

The estate planning choices of actor Philip Seymour Hoffman, who passed away in 2014, offer an instructive example. Intentionally avoiding trusts to prevent his children from becoming "trust fund kids," he instead left his estate to his longtime partner to manage for their benefit. While well-intentioned, this approach resulted in a substantial estate tax liability—one that could have been mitigated with more strategic use of trusts.

Hoffman's story underscores the delicate balance between personal values and financial prudence in estate planning. It highlights how well-crafted trusts can simultaneously protect assets for beneficiaries and minimize tax burdens.

Fulfilling The Trustee's Final Responsibilities

Trustees carry the vital responsibility of managing and settling the trust efficiently and transparently. A detailed checklist can serve as a crucial tool to guide trustees through the process, ensuring no essential steps are overlooked.

Initial Steps:

- **Review the Trust Document:** Fully understand the trust's terms, trustee duties, and beneficiaries' rights.
- **Notify Beneficiaries:** Officially inform all beneficiaries about the trust's activation and their role in the process.

- **Inventory Assets:** Compile a complete list of trust assets, noting their value and location.

Administration Phase:

- **Obtain Appraisals:** Seek professional valuations for valuable assets to assess the trust's total worth accurately.
- **Manage Assets Prudently:** Invest and oversee assets in accordance with the trust's terms, aiming to preserve or enhance their value.
- **Settle Debts and Taxes:** Pay any outstanding debts and taxes before distributing assets.

Legal and Financial Compliance:

- **File Tax Returns:** Ensure all required trust tax filings are completed in a timely manner.
- **Maintain Detailed Records:** Keep comprehensive documentation of transactions, income, expenses, and distributions.
- **Communicate Regularly:** Keep beneficiaries updated on the trust's status and important developments.

Distribution Phase:

- **Plan Distribution Schedule:** Establish a clear timeline for asset distribution as dictated by the trust.
- **Distribute Assets:** Transfer assets fairly and accurately to beneficiaries.
- **Prepare Final Accounting:** Provide beneficiaries with a detailed report of all financial activity and distributions.

Closing Actions:

- **Obtain Releases:** Secure written acknowledgment from beneficiaries confirming satisfaction with the administration.
- **Close the Trust:** Formally conclude the trust's administration once all duties are fulfilled.

This checklist helps trustees carry out their duties diligently, with integrity, and in full alignment with the trustor's wishes.

Navigating Difficult Decisions as a Trustee

Trustees often face challenging decisions requiring a balance of empathy, legal insight, and fidelity to the trust's intent. Here are strategies to approach these complexities:

- **Master the Trust Document:** The foundation of all decisions is the trust itself. Familiarity with its language ensures decisions align with the trustor's intentions and legal requirements.
- **Seek Professional Guidance:** When confronted with complicated or high-stakes choices, consult legal and financial experts to clarify issues and reduce risks.
- **Communicate Transparently:** Keeping beneficiaries informed about decisions and their rationale fosters trust and can prevent conflicts.
- **Document Decision Processes:** Maintain thorough records of decisions, including the data reviewed and advice received, to provide accountability and defense if disputes arise.
- **Consider Mediation:** When disagreements occur, mediation with a neutral third party can often resolve disputes without costly litigation.

- **Prioritize Fairness and Integrity:** Always act impartially and in the best interests of all beneficiaries, honoring the trustor's legacy.

With these strategies, trustees can confidently manage difficult situations while fulfilling their fiduciary responsibilities.

The Astor Estate Battle: A Cautionary Tale

The protracted legal battle over Brooke Astor's estate reveals how unclear or outdated trust documents can lead to costly disputes. Accusations of undue influence over Astor in her later years led to a public and expensive court fight, damaging her legacy and family relationships.

This case serves as a powerful reminder of the need for clear, precise, and regularly updated estate planning documents—especially in situations where mental capacity may decline. Well-drafted trusts help prevent challenges and protect the trustor's intentions.

How Trustees Can Avoid Legal Landmines

Trustees must be vigilant to avoid common pitfalls that could expose them to legal challenges or jeopardize the trust's integrity:

- **Adhere Strictly to the Trust Document:** Never deviate from the trust's terms without proper legal guidance.
- **Maintain Detailed Records:** Document every transaction and communication meticulously to defend against accusations of mismanagement.

- **Uphold Fiduciary Duties:** Act solely in beneficiaries' best interests, avoiding conflicts of interest and ensuring prudent asset management.
- **Communicate Clearly and Regularly:** Transparent communication builds beneficiary trust and reduces the likelihood of disputes.
- **Avoid Unnecessary Delays:** Distribute assets promptly once obligations are met to prevent frustration and legal action.

By proactively managing these areas and seeking professional advice when needed, trustees can navigate estate settlement safely and effectively.

Key Takeaways

- **Clear Communication Is Essential:** Keeping beneficiaries well-informed throughout administration fosters transparency and prevents misunderstandings.
- **Know the Trust Document Inside and Out:** Trustees must base their actions on the trust's terms to honor the trustor's intent and comply with legal requirements.
- **Manage Assets Proactively:** Timely inventory, valuation, and prudent investment help preserve or grow the estate's value.
- **Comply Fully with Legal and Tax Obligations:** Paying debts, taxes, and expenses before distributions protects against legal complications.
- **Avoid Legal Pitfalls:** Awareness and proactive management reduce risks related to breaches of fiduciary duty or mismanagement.
- **Aim for Efficient, Fair Settlement:** The goal is to transfer assets smoothly and fairly, respecting the trustor's wishes and minimizing conflict.

Through careful administration, trustees can uphold the trustor's legacy and provide beneficiaries with a seamless transition.

Final Thoughts

As we come to the close of this journey through trusts and estate planning, it's worth pausing to reflect on how much ground we've covered together. Each chapter has been a deliberate step toward demystifying trusts and transforming what often feels like an overwhelming subject into something practical, understandable, and empowering.

Throughout this book, you've explored living trusts, tax considerations, beneficiary protections, and the growing importance of digital asset management. What may have once seemed complex or intimidating is now a structured set of tools you can use to take control of your financial future. These insights are not merely theoretical—they are actionable building blocks designed to help you create an estate plan that reflects your values, protects your loved ones, and preserves your legacy.

By understanding and strategically applying the principles of trust planning, you've positioned yourself to make informed decisions that endure beyond your lifetime. Estate planning is not just about preparing for the end—it's about bringing clarity, stability, and peace of mind to the present.

Summarizing Retirement & Estate Planning with Trusts

The strategies and concepts explored throughout this book reveal several essential themes that together form a comprehensive approach to retirement and estate planning.

The Foundation of Living Trusts
You were introduced to the purpose, structure, and flexibility of living trusts, along with the different types available and the critical roles they play in long-term planning.

Demystifying Common Misconceptions
We addressed and dismantled common myths surrounding trusts, revealing that they are not exclusive tools for the wealthy but practical solutions accessible to individuals and families at many stages of life.

The Advantages of Trust Planning
Trusts offer meaningful benefits, including probate avoidance, enhanced privacy, asset control, and smoother transitions for beneficiaries—advantages that traditional estate plans often lack.

Trusts as a Core Estate Planning Tool
You explored how trusts fit into a broader estate strategy, supporting tax efficiency, protecting assets, and accommodating modern considerations such as digital property.

Digital Asset Management in a Modern World
As our lives increasingly move online, the importance of planning for digital assets and digital legacies has become

essential. You've learned how trusts can adapt to protect these evolving forms of wealth.

Trust Administration Essentials
From trustee responsibilities to beneficiary communication, the book outlined what effective trust administration looks like and how careful management helps avoid disputes and legal pitfalls.

Tax Implications and Planning Strategies
You gained insight into how trusts interact with estate, income, and gift taxes—and how thoughtful planning can reduce tax burdens for both the estate and its beneficiaries.

Beneficiary Considerations
Timing, method of distribution, and tax consequences all play a role in inheritance outcomes. Understanding these factors helps ensure that beneficiaries receive assets efficiently and responsibly.

Recognizing Challenges and Risks
No planning tool is without limitations. By identifying potential drawbacks and risks in trust planning, you're better prepared to address them proactively and strengthen your overall plan.

Post-Death Administration
Finally, you explored the steps that follow a trustor's death, gaining clarity on how trusts function in practice to fulfill final wishes and bring closure to the estate.

Together, these themes form a practical blueprint—one that allows you to approach retirement and estate planning with confidence rather than uncertainty.

With the knowledge and strategies you've gained, the path forward is clear. The next step is action. Begin implementing your estate plan, review it regularly, and refine it as life evolves. When questions arise or complexities surface, don't hesitate to seek guidance from qualified legal and financial professionals.

If this book has helped clarify your thinking or influenced your planning, consider sharing your experience by leaving a review on Amazon. Your insight can encourage and empower others to take charge of their own estate planning journey.

And remember—every proactive step you take today is an investment in the future you want to protect.

Living Trusts A–Z: Glossary of Key Terms

Annual Exclusion
The maximum amount of money or value a person may give to another individual in a single year without triggering federal gift tax or reducing the lifetime gift and estate tax exemption.

Asset
Anything of value owned or controlled by an individual, trust, or business, including property, cash, investments, and digital property.

Beneficiary
A person or organization entitled to receive assets, income, or benefits from a trust, will, life insurance policy, or retirement account.

Charitable Remainder Trust (CRT)
A tax-exempt, irrevocable trust that provides income to one or more beneficiaries for a set period, after which the remaining assets are donated to a designated charity.

Conservator
An individual or institution appointed by a court to manage the financial or personal affairs of someone who is unable to do so themselves due to incapacity.

Digital Assets
Electronic information or property that exists in digital form and carries ownership or usage rights, including emails, photographs, social media accounts, online businesses, and cryptocurrencies.

Estate Planning
The process of organizing and arranging how an individual's assets will be managed, protected, and distributed in the event of incapacity or death.

Estate Tax
A tax imposed on the transfer of a deceased person's estate before assets are distributed to beneficiaries.

Executor
The person or institution appointed in a will to carry out the deceased person's final wishes, including settling debts and distributing assets.

Gift Tax
A federal tax applied when an individual transfers money or property to another person without receiving full value in return.

Grantor
The person who creates a trust and transfers assets into it; also referred to as the trustor or settlor.

Guardian
An individual legally appointed to care for the personal, financial, or medical needs of a minor or an adult who cannot manage their own affairs.

Heir
A person legally entitled to inherit property from a deceased individual, typically when no will or trust specifies otherwise.

Inheritance Tax
A tax imposed on individuals who receive money or property from a deceased person's estate. Unlike estate tax,

this tax is paid by the beneficiary and applies only in certain jurisdictions.

Irrevocable Trust
A trust that generally cannot be changed, amended, or terminated once it has been created, except under limited circumstances and with beneficiary consent.

Living Trust
A legal arrangement created during an individual's lifetime in which assets are placed into a trust to be managed for the grantor's benefit and later distributed to beneficiaries, often avoiding probate.

Pour-Over Will
A will that directs any assets not already placed in a living trust at the time of death to be transferred into the trust, ensuring consistency in asset distribution.

Probate
The court-supervised legal process of validating a will, paying debts and taxes, and distributing a deceased person's assets to heirs or beneficiaries.

Revocable Trust
A trust that can be modified, amended, or revoked by the grantor during their lifetime, offering flexibility and control over trust assets.

Trustee
An individual or institution responsible for managing trust assets according to the terms of the trust and in the best interests of the beneficiaries.

Will
A legal document that outlines how a person's property

should be distributed after death and names the individual or entity responsible for carrying out those instructions.

About the Author

Dr. Mike Brandon is an educator and advocate for practical estate planning, dedicated to helping individuals and families protect their assets, avoid unnecessary legal complications, and preserve their legacies with clarity and confidence. His work focuses on simplifying complex topics such as living trusts, probate avoidance, tax planning, and digital asset management, making them accessible to everyday readers.

With a strong belief that estate planning is not just for the wealthy, Dr. Brandon emphasizes proactive planning, informed decision-making, and clear communication as the foundations of effective legacy protection. His writing blends practical guidance with real-world examples to help readers take meaningful action.

Dr. Brandon is particularly interested in modern estate planning challenges, including digital privacy and the evolving nature of wealth in a technology-driven world. Through his work, he encourages readers to approach estate planning not as a legal burden, but as a thoughtful act of responsibility and care for future generations.

References & Citations

1. American Bar Association. *Estate Planning Basics.* American Bar Association Publishing.

2. Internal Revenue Service (IRS). *Estate and Gift Taxes.* IRS Publications 525, 559, 706, and 709.

3. Internal Revenue Service (IRS). *Distributions from Trusts and Estates.* IRS Publication 544.

4. Uniform Law Commission. *Uniform Trust Code (UTC).* National Conference of Commissioners on Uniform State Laws.

5. U.S. Securities and Exchange Commission (SEC). *Investor Bulletin: Estate Planning.*

6. Nolo Editors. *Living Trusts: Everything You Need to Know.* Nolo Press.

7. Sitkoff, Robert H., and Jesse Dukeminier. *Wills, Trusts, and Estates.* Wolters Kluwer Law & Business.

8. Langbein, John H. *The Nonprobate Revolution and the Future of the Law of Succession.* Harvard Law Review.

9. Federal Trade Commission (FTC). *Identity Theft and Digital Privacy Guidance.*

10. European Union. *General Data Protection Regulation (GDPR).* Regulation (EU) 2016/679.

11. California Consumer Privacy Act (CCPA). California Civil Code §1798.100 et seq.

12. Coinbase Institutional. *Cryptocurrency Custody and Estate Planning Considerations.*

13. Fidelity Investments. *Estate Planning and Trust Administration Insights.*

14. Schwab Center for Financial Research. *Trusts and Estate Planning Strategies.*

15. CNBC, Forbes, and Bloomberg Wealth. Coverage on high-profile estate cases including:

- B.B. King Estate Dispute
- Philip Seymour Hoffman Estate
- Brooke Astor Estate Litigation
- Walton Family Trust Structures

Author’s Note on Citations

This book is written for educational purposes and practical understanding. Laws governing trusts, taxes, and estate planning vary by jurisdiction and may change over time. Readers are encouraged to consult licensed estate planning attorneys, tax professionals, or financial advisors for advice tailored to their specific circumstances.

www.ingramcontent.com/pod-product-compliance
Lightning Source LLC
Chambersburg PA
CBHW041300210926
51847CB00009B/86
9781957141800